jQuery 1.3 with PHP

Enhance your PHP applications by increasing their responsiveness through jQuery and its plugins

Kae Verens

BIRMINGHAM - MUMBAI

jQuery 1.3 with PHP

First published: October 2009

Production Reference: 1211009

Published by Packt Publishing Ltd.
32 Lincoln Road
Olton
Birmingham, B27 6PA, UK.

ISBN 978-1-847196-98-9

www.packtpub.com

Cover Image by Louise Barr (lou@frogboxdesign.co.uk)

Credits

Author
Kae Verens

Reviewers
Akash Mehta

Ashok Modi

John K. Murphy

Acquisition Editor
Douglas Paterson

Development Editor
Darshana D. Shinde

Technical Editor
Ishita Dhabalia

Copy Editor
Sanchari Mukherjee

Editorial Team Leader
Gagandeep Singh

Project Team Leader
Lata Basantani

Project Coordinator
Srimoyee Ghoshal

Proofreader
Chris Smith

Indexer
Rekha Nair

Production Coordinator
Dolly Dasilva

Cover Work
Dolly Dasilva

About the Author

Kae Verens lives in Monaghan, Ireland with his wife Bronwyn and their two kids Jareth and Boann. He has been programming for twenty years, fifteen of which were as a professional.

Kae started writing in JavaScript in the mid nineties, and started working on the server-side languages a few years later. After writing CGI in C and Perl, Kae switched to PHP in 2000, and has worked with it since then.

Kae is currently the secretary of the Irish PHP Users' Group, `http://php.ie/`, is part-owner of the Irish web-development company Webworks.ie, `http://webworks.ie/`, and is the author of popular web-based file-manager KFM, `http://kfm.verens.com/`.

In his spare time, Kae plays the guitar, juggles, is learning to play the piano, and likes to occasionally dust the skateboard off and mess around on it.

I would like to thank Packt Publishing for considering me for this project; it's been a journey, and I've learned quite a lot from it. I would also like to thank Webworks.ie for hiring me way back in 2001, when I was a brash programmer, eager to show how things should be done. And finally, I'd like to thank Bronwyn and the kids for putting up with the days and hours that I've had to avoid them to concentrate on the book!

About the Reviewers

Akash Mehta is a web application developer and technical author based in Australia. His area of work covers e-learning solutions, information systems, and developer training. He regularly writes web development articles for Adobe, CNet, the APC Magazine, and other print and online publications. He is a regular speaker at IT conferences, user groups, and BarCamps. Currently, Akash provides various services like web development, technical writing, consulting, and training through his website, `http://bitmeta.org/`.

Hailing from an igloo somewhere up in Canada, **Ashok Modi** is currently a systems analyst for California Institute of the Arts (`http://calarts.edu/`). He was a systems (and games) programmer for zinc Roe Design (`http://www.zincroe.com/`), and has been working with Drupal for the last three years. Starting from Drupal 4.6, he is the author of the abuse module (and looking for co-maintainers!), and has helped many maintainers in updating their contributed modules from 4.7.x to 5.x to 6.x. He also helped organize DrupalCamp Toronto in 2007 and 2008 and recently presented multiple sessions at DrupalCamp LA in 2009. In his spare time, Ashok tries to help contributed module maintainers with features and bugs. He was a technical reviewer on another book, *Drupal 6 Social Networking*, also published by *Packt Publishing*.

> I would like to thank my wife, Richa, for letting me obsess over technology and pushing me to freelance and try other open-source technologies in my spare time.

John K. Murphy is a graduate of the University of West Virginia and has been wrapped up in computers and software development since the 1980s. When he is not buried in a book or jumping out of an airplane, he works as an IT consultant.

John lives with his wife and two children in Pittsburgh, PA and is currently obsessing about the Internet of Things.

Table of Contents

Preface

Creating PHP applications that respond quickly, avoid unnecessary page reloads, and provide great user interfaces, often requires complex JavaScript techniques. Even then, if you get that far, the results might not work across different browsers! With jQuery, you can use one of the most popular JavaScript libraries, forget about cross-browser issues, and simplify the creation of very powerful and responsive interfaces — all with the minimum of code.

This is the first book in the market that will ease the server-side PHP coder into the client-side world of the popular jQuery JavaScript library.

This book will show you how to use jQuery to enhance your PHP applications, with many examples using jQuery's user interface library jQuery UI, and other examples using popular jQuery plugins. It will help you to add exciting user interface features to liven up your PHP applications without having to become a master of client-side JavaScript.

This book will teach you how to use jQuery to create some really stunning effects, but without you needing to have in-depth knowledge of how jQuery works. It provides you with everything you need to build practical user interfaces, for everything from graphics manipulation and drag-and-drop to data searching, and much more. The book also provides practical demonstrations of PHP and jQuery and explains these examples, rather than starting from how JavaScript works and how it is different from PHP.

By the end of this book, you should be able to take any PHP application you have written, and transform it into a responsive, user-friendly interface, with capabilities you would not have dreamed of being able to achieve, all in just a few lines of JavaScript.

What this book covers

Chapter 1, *Introduction and Overview*, introduces you to what jQuery is, why you would want to use it, and why is it useful to combine it with PHP. Also, it gives a list of projects illustrating uses for combining PHP and jQuery.

Chapter 2, *Quick Tricks*, looks at a few quick examples on how to interface PHP and jQuery and a few tricks, which demonstrate how to relieve the most obvious resource wastes on the server.

Chapter 3, *Tabs and Accordions*, walks through the creation of tabs and accordions using the jQuery UI project, managing tabs and accordions using a rich text editor and a bit of PHP, and using Ajax to populate your accordion and tab panels.

Chapter 4, *Forms and Form Validation*, explores form validation using jQuery and PHP and how to use the same PHP configuration to validate on both sides — the server and the client side. It also covers examples on optimization of large select boxes and building auto-suggest fields.

Chapter 5, *File Management*, teaches you to manage almost everything — creating, uploading, editing, moving, downloading, and deleting files and directories.

Chapter 6, *Calendars*, builds a weekly calendar for you, which has events that can be created, edited, moved around, and deleted. It also takes care of recurring events.

Chapter 7, *Image Manipulation*, discusses methods for manipulating images with jQuery and PHP, along with some ways to make the changes non-destructive, so that multiple manipulations, such as select, rotate, resize, and crop, can be made on the same image.

Chapter 8, *Drag and Drop*, demonstrates a few uses of drag and drop, including sorting lists, dragging between lists, and hierarchical sorting, which can be used to improve the usability of your content management system.

Chapter 9, *Data Tables*, builds a very large data table and discusses how to navigate, sort, search, paginate, and search it using jQuery and Ajax.

Chapter 10, *Optimization*, shows the ways to optimize jQuery and various other elements of the web development environment.

What you need for this book

To try out the examples in this book, all you need is a test server; we recommend using PHP 5.2 or up. You will also need to download the jQuery library from http://docs.jquery.com/Downloading_jQuery.

Who this book is for

This book is for PHP application developers who want to improve their user interfaces through jQuery's capabilities and responsiveness. Whether you are familiar with jQuery or have only dabbled a little with JavaScript, this book will provide you with numerous practical examples on how to improve your application.

Conventions

In this book, you will find a number of styles of text that distinguish between different kinds of information. Here are some examples of these styles, and an explanation of their meaning.

Code words in text are shown as follows: "The URL string we're working with includes a number of sSearch parameters."

A block of code is set as follows:

```php
<?php
  $dir='.'; // directory containing the scripts
  $d=0;
  foreach (new DirectoryIterator($dir) as $file) {
    $d+=$file->getMTime();
  }
?>
```

When we wish to draw your attention to a particular part of a code block, the relevant lines or items are set in bold:

```
$.getJSON('./calendar.php?action=get_event&id='+calEvent.id,
  function(eventdata){
    var controls='<a href="javascript:calendar_delete_entry('
                          +eventdata.id+');">'
                +'[delete]</a>';
    if(+eventdata.recurring)controls+='<br />'
      +'<a href="javascript:calendar_delete_recurrences('
              +eventdata.id+')">'
      +'  [stop recurring]</a>';
        $('<div id="calendar_edit_entry_form"
```

Any command-line input or output is written as follows:

```
yum install php-pecl-imagick
```

New terms and **important words** are shown in bold. Words that you see on the screen, in menus or dialog boxes for example, appear in the text like this: "When you click on this **?** icon, smaller help icons will be shown next to all the elements in the page."

 Warnings or important notes appear in a box like this.

 Tips and tricks appear like this.

Reader feedback

Feedback from our readers is always welcome. Let us know what you think about this book—what you liked or may have disliked. Reader feedback is important for us to develop titles that you really get the most out of.

To send us general feedback, simply send an email to feedback@packtpub.com, and mention the book title via the subject of your message.

If there is a book that you need and would like to see us publish, please send us a note in the **SUGGEST A TITLE** form on www.packtpub.com or email suggest@packtpub.com.

If there is a topic that you have expertise in and you are interested in either writing or contributing to a book, see our author guide on www.packtpub.com/authors.

Customer support

Now that you are the proud owner of a Packt book, we have a number of things to help you to get the most from your purchase.

 Downloading the example code for the book
Visit http://www.packtpub.com/files/code/6989_Code.zip to directly download the example code.

Errata

Although we have taken every care to ensure the accuracy of our content, mistakes do happen. If you find a mistake in one of our books—maybe a mistake in the text or the code—we would be grateful if you would report this to us. By doing so, you can save other readers from frustration, and help us to improve subsequent versions of this book. If you find any errata, please report them by visiting http://www.packtpub.com/support, selecting your book, clicking on the **let us know** link, and entering the details of your errata. Once your errata are verified, your submission will be accepted and the errata added to any list of existing errata. Any existing errata can be viewed by selecting your title from http://www.packtpub.com/support.

Piracy

Piracy of copyright material on the Internet is an ongoing problem across all media. At Packt, we take the protection of our copyright and licenses very seriously. If you come across any illegal copies of our works, in any form, on the Internet, please provide us with the location address or web site name immediately so that we can pursue a remedy.

Please contact us at copyright@packtpub.com with a link to the suspected pirated material.

We appreciate your help in protecting our authors, and our ability to bring you valuable content.

Questions

You can contact us at questions@packtpub.com if you are having a problem with any aspect of the book, and we will do our best to address it.

1
Introduction and Overview

Welcome!

This book is a general overview of how to take advantage of jQuery's ease-of-use to make your PHP applications more "snappy" on the client side.

The book is aimed at the PHP developers who usually don't write client-side JavaScript, and would like an example-based introduction demonstrating a wide variety of integrations between server-side and client-side code.

For years, JavaScript (the language that jQuery is written in) has been seen as a "toy" language. However, the pervasiveness of Ajax has allowed it to break out of the client side and become an essential tool for all serious web application developers.

Ajax is a tool used by client-side code to contact the server and get or send data without needing to reload the entire page. It's used to update part of the page, or to retrieve data for a JavaScript application, or to send data to the server. Ajax stands for **Asynchronous JavaScript And XML**. However, the XML part is optional, and is often replaced with plain text or another data format such as **JSON** (explained later in this chapter).

This book will demonstrate how combining server-side PHP with client-side jQuery can make JavaScript much more useful than just for "form checking".

It is assumed that you are a server-side web application developer who wants to take a step into the client side and learn how to use JavaScript to make your applications more efficient and exciting for the client.

To be very clear about it, this book is not about PHP, and it is not about jQuery — it is about how to work with *both* PHP and jQuery. This book will teach you how to use jQuery to create some really cool effects, but without you needing to have in-depth knowledge of how jQuery works.

With this book, we are more interested in providing some practical demonstrations of PHP and jQuery with explanations, than in getting right down into the guts of how JavaScript works and how it is different from PHP.

After reading this book, you will have seen and built a wide variety of example applications. This would certainly be enough to immensely change how your current PHP applications work.

Each chapter in this book is dedicated to a specific subject, and will usually involve building a practical example, which you can use in your day-to-day work.

Expected developer skills

To read and work with this book's contents, it is expected that you are already a PHP developer with a basic understanding of JavaScript, and experience of HTML and CSS.

The book will not cover jQuery in depth—there are other books available that are dedicated to it. This book is designed to help a PHP developer write some immediately-useful client-side applications without needing weeks of study.

You need to understand how CSS selectors work. A CSS selector is the part of CSS that goes to the left of the { character. jQuery selects elements by using CSS selectors, and it's an extremely powerful way of choosing the elements that you wish to work on.

HTML is a must-have for every web developer. I think we can safely say that your HTML skills are not lacking, especially because that's the environment that PHP is usually working in.

Your PHP is expected to be good. You don't need to know everything about PHP, but it is beneficial if you have already written a few full PHP projects yourself and are comfortable with reading code and quickly understanding what it does.

You are not expected to be a good JavaScript writer. It will be useful, but the book is written such that beginners should not have a problem understanding how it all fits together. As a PHP developer, you will find that JavaScript is similar to PHP anyway, so you should not have a problem reading the examples and understanding them.

Differences between PHP and JavaScript

Syntactically, JavaScript and PHP are very similar. They're both **loosely typed** languages, and you can choose whether to write in an object-oriented or functional way.

However, there are some interesting differences, which a PHP developer may not have encountered before.

One example is asynchronous events. In PHP, everything happens linearly—when you call a function, the result is returned before the next line runs. However, in JavaScript, you can call some functions and have them return their results to a "callback" function a few seconds later.

The most obvious example is Ajax: when you request information from the server, it is bad design to have everything freeze while you're waiting for the data to return. Instead, you write your script such that the data is sent, and you carry on with other stuff. When the data returns, you handle it with another function.

This poses some interesting problems, such as race conditions, and how to pass variables through to remind the script what it was supposed to be doing when the Ajax request was fired.

A race condition occurs when one resource is accessed by two separate operations at the same time and one of them changes the value. This is because computers always do things one after the other; the change to the value will happen either before or after the other operation. This uncertainty means that in asynchronous systems, such as networks, care must be taken to make sure that things happen in the right order.

Race conditions are not a language-specific problem. They can happen anytime—say, when you open a file, work on it, and close it, only to find that at the time you were working on it, someone else came in and changed the name of the file. There are many ways of solving these problems depending on the nature of the case. The most common solution is to use a "lock", where if an operation is to write into a value, it will first "lock" it (usually by setting a flag variable or creating a `.lock` file) before it reads it, and then will "unlock" it (remove the file or unset the flag) after it has completed its work.

When an asynchronous function is called and its return value is sent to a callback function, that callback function must be reminded what the caller function was doing, so that it can carry on with it. This can be done using **closures**. With closures, the callback function is generated by the caller function, and has a copy of the caller's environment, including what variables were set, among other things. Later in the book, you will see some examples of this.

What is jQuery?

jQuery is a JavaScript library that makes it easy to work with the **Document Object Model (DOM)** of a website. jQuery is not a replacement for JavaScript. It is a JavaScript library, which gives some extra functionality that is not available natively in JavaScript itself.

jQuery is designed to make it easy to create, manipulate, or destroy elements in the document. Manipulation includes animation, CSS effects such as fades, resizes, and so on.

jQuery also makes it very easy to add behaviors to elements. So, you can do things like drag boxes around, have things happen when you hover a mouse cursor over something, have scripts run when a select box is changed, and so on.

All of this can be accomplished in plain JavaScript if you feel the need to write it yourself, but there is no point in re-inventing the wheel. If there is a tool available that makes things easier for you, then you should not do it the hard way.

Besides, handwritten JavaScript tends to be much more verbose than it could be if you used a library, such as jQuery.

As an example, let's say that you want to get all of the `<span>` elements in a page that are contained in an element with the `testme` class, and change their contents to the word **hi!**. Here is the HTML of the example:

```
<html>
  <head>
  </head>
  <body>
    <h1 class="testme"><span>this will change</span></h1>
    <p>this will not</p>
    <p class="testme">this will also not</p>
    <p class="testme"><span>this will change</span></p>
    <a href="javascript:run_test()">do it</a>
  </body>
</html>
```

When displayed in a browser, it will look like the following:

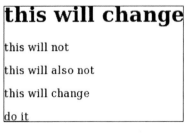

When the **do it** link is clicked, we want the view to change to this:

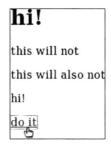

For the first test, here is how to do it in plain JavaScript. Place this code in the `<head>` section of the previous HTML code.

```
<script>
  function run_test(){
    var i,j,els,els2;
    els=document.getElementsByTagName('*');
    for(i in els){
      if(!/(^| )testme( |$)/.test(els[i].className))continue;
      els2=els[i].getElementsByTagName('span');
      for(j in els2){
        els2[j].innerHTML='hi!';
      }
    }
  }
</script>
```

It would be difficult to write this more compactly in pure JavaScript, but it's still too complex to be maintainable. Really, if you saw that for the first time, would you know straight away what it was trying to do? And, can you be sure that it will work in all browsers?

With jQuery, you can write a much more readable piece of code. Replace the above JavaScript with this:

```
<script src="../jquery.min.js"></script>
<script>
  function run_test(){
    $('.testme span').html('hi!');
  }
</script>
```

I know what you're thinking—where's the rest of it? Well, that's the whole thing. It very concisely strips away the confusion and all that you end up with is a very clear piece of code, which can be understood immediately. The problems of cross-browser compatibility are also solved by using the jQuery library. You can be sure that the new script will work as planned in all major browsers.

The example links to the jQuery library file, `jquery.min.js`, which you can download from `http://jqueryjs.googlecode.com/files/jquery-1.3.2.min.js`.

Why jQuery?

There are many libraries and frameworks available for JavaScript, including MooTools, Ext, Dojo, and Prototype. So, why use jQuery and not others? Here are some of the reasons:

- jQuery has a huge number of plugins available for everything you could imagine wanting to do online
- The information on the jQuery site is extremely well documented, with many examples
- jQuery does not extend the elements that it works on, which means that JavaScript such as `'for(i in el){...}'` will still work
- jQuery's CSS selector engine, **Sizzle**, is arguably the most complete and the quickest available

jQuery is available at Google's Ajax Libs CDN (`http://code.google.com/apis/ajaxlibs`), so probably you already have it in your browser's cache.

There are benefits and detractors to everything. So in the end, it's a matter of taste.

In my case, I was using MooTools before I turned to jQuery, but MooTools' habit of extending every element it touches was interfering with my own code, so I had to replace it.

I chose jQuery because the body of knowledge on it was very large (every second article on JavaScript blogs appears to mention jQuery), it's impressively clean to work with, and there are a massive number of plugins available.

Also, because jQuery is used in so many large projects (a few of which are mentioned in the *Projects that use PHP and jQuery* section of this chapter). If you have ever worked on any of those projects, you will find that the skills you learned on them are transferable to other projects using jQuery.

How does jQuery fit in with PHP?

Traditional network applications have both server and client side, each of which is a program in its own right.

As a very simple example, consider a networked game, where you are playing against a number of other people. The server holds a database of the present positions of everything, and decides if something is allowed or not. On each player's computer, there is a client, which gets data from the server and displays it in a user-friendly way, such as rendering a 3D world that you can move around in. The client is smart enough that if you try to do something that is obviously not allowed, such as run through a wall, then it won't let you.

It would be silly if a 3D screen was generated on the server and was sent to the client 24 times per second. And it would be awkward if you tried to do something like walk through a wall, and had to wait for the server to decide if it was allowed or not.

However, in a pure PHP environment, that's exactly what has been happening—the server generates absolutely everything that the client displays. If an element needs to be removed from a table, for example, then the server needs to be told, so that it can give the client the new view. If you try to do something illegal, such as submit a blank form where an email address is required, then pure PHP applications will let you do that, wasting time and server resources.

However, using JavaScript, and especially using Ajax, the client side is no longer a "dumb terminal" for the server. We can write applications fully on the client side, if we wish, using the server purely as a database. This book will demonstrate ways to work towards that.

Although Ajax stands for Asynchronous JavaScript And XML, it's a misnomer. This is because in most cases, no XML is involved (either plain HTML or data in JSON format is usually used). Ajax allows a client to open a data channel between itself and the server, allowing JavaScript to load new information from the server without needing to refresh the entire screen.

JSON stands for **JavaScript Object Notation**. It is a simple data storage format, which can be used to transfer information about strings, numbers, arrays, and associative arrays between various languages. It is much smaller than XML, and is much easier to transform because there is a direct relationship between the text format and the internal data format. It can be used in both PHP and JavaScript. It's based on how JavaScript is actually written, so it can be natively compiled into an object in JavaScript.

In JavaScript, you can create an actual data object from JSON by simply "eval"ing it (or using the new `json.decode` function in newer browsers). In PHP, you can use the `json_decode` and `json_encode` functions to convert from and to JSON.

With Ajax, we can provide a client-side experience, which had only been possible beforehand using external plugins, such as Java or Flash. It could not safely be assumed that these plugins were available on the client. Every major browser now supports Ajax, so there are much fewer reasons to rely on proprietary technology these days.

jQuery simplifies Ajax. With pure Ajax, you need to do low-level stuff like create an `XMLHTTPRequest` object (taking care of cross-browser incompatibilities), set callbacks, check response values, and so on. With jQuery, all you need to do is use `$.get` or one of the other jQuery JSON functions. These functions will take care of the low-level stuff for you.

How to work with the examples

In every chapter of this book, I will provide a few code examples. If you wish to try them out, you will need to replicate the test environment I'm using here.

On my test server, my directory layout (within the `public_html` directory) is like this:

```
./php_and_jquery
./php_and_jquery/jquery.min.js
./php_and_jquery/jquery-ui.css
./php_and_jquery/jquery-ui.min.js
./php_and_jquery/1-tests
./php_and_jquery/2-contextual_help
[... others from various chapters ...]
./php_and_jquery/ckeditor
./php_and_jquery/images
./php_and_jquery/jquery-validate
[... other plugins ...]
```

You can see that there's a common theme—everything has its own subdirectory. The jQuery library is kept in the root directory, `./php_and_jquery/`, along with the jQuery UI library (when we use it). We will discuss where to get these from in Chapter 2, *Quick Tricks*.

Here is the root directory of my own test server. It shows the libraries we will use throughout the book, and two test directories (9-5 and 9-4):

When creating your own test server, it should end up looking like this.

You can start out with the empty directories. Each chapter will explain what new files to download and where to get them from.

Each of the examples has a number of screenshots, so you can verify your own tests against what my tests display.

Projects that use PHP and jQuery

Here is a small list of projects that use jQuery along with PHP. This illustrates the variety of uses that jQuery is put to.

WordPress

WordPress (`http://wordpress.org/`) is probably the best-known blogging software on the net. Recently, the admin dashboard area was given a thorough going over, and is now extremely flexible with the areas you can move around or remove, a navigation menu you can hide at the click of a button, and other improvements. jQuery is used to handle autosaves, word counts, and much more.

RoundCube

RoundCube (`http://roundcube.net/`) allows you to read your emails online using an application designed to look similar to your normal email client. With jQuery, the engine allows emails to be removed, moved around, and so on, without reloading the whole page.

[Roundcube webmail interface screenshot]

KFM

I'm proud to say that this is one of my own projects. KFM (`http://kfm.verens.com/`) is a file manager, which allows you to upload, sort, and rename (and more) your files online. You can even edit text files or play media files. The project is designed to look like a desktop file manager, complete with file icons, tree directory, and so on. jQuery is used for most of it.

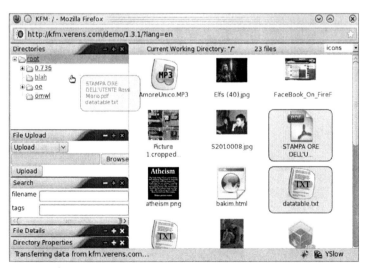

Drupal

Drupal (`http://drupal.org/`) is a Content Management System. Since version 5, jQuery has been included as part of the core. It's more prominently used in some of the modules, but some core functionality, such as story creation is enhanced by allowing text boxes to be re-sized, optional sections to be hidden/shown, and so on.

Now, without further ado, let's get on with the fun stuff.

Summary

In this chapter, we discussed what jQuery is, why you would want to use it, and why is it useful to combine it with PHP.

We also saw a list of projects illustrating some uses for combining PHP and jQuery.

In the next chapter, we will look at a few examples of how you can use jQuery immediately to give your site a more "live" feel, without needing to know a lot of JavaScript.

2
Quick Tricks

PHP programmers can be tempted to consider only the server side of the website equation and leave the client side to the designer. Your job, as a PHP developer, is to make sure that the requested actions happen efficiently, and this does not appear to be a client-side problem.

When a customer expresses that the site doesn't look very modern or snappy, as a server-side developer, it is tempting to think that this is a problem for the designers, as they have traditionally had most of the control about what is sent to the client, and you have traditionally only been asked to supply an HTML skeleton for them to wrap the design around.

However, more and more code these days is shifting onto the client side of the transaction. And as a result, developers are taking a stronger interest in how they can affect data on the client side, and how they can help the designer to make an impact.

There are reasons why you, as a developer, should be interested in what happens on the client side. Using tricks such as Ajax and client-side form validation, you can relieve the strain on bandwidth and the server's resources, and at the same time, increase the responsiveness and usability of the application.

What happens on the client side does affect the server side. It is optimizing of this overlap, and not heavy and centralized architectures, that can help your own application scale with more ease.

And that's partly what's different about PHP/HTML versus PHP/HTML/jQuery. In the old PHP/HTML architecture, we had a very clear distinction, where data was calculated and turned into HTML on the server, and the client was used just for displaying that data exactly as the server rendered it. However, we are now at a point where we can use the power of client-side technologies, such as jQuery, to do part of the rendering on the client.

This allows your systems to grow easily, but it also allows your clients to have more control over how the data is rendered on the screen. With PHP and jQuery, your users will learn how quick and tactile their interfaces are, your marketers will love the "wow factor" that happens when they show the system to new customers, and your administrators will love you for relieving the burden on the server that classic "web 1.0" methods impose.

As PHP is used at the server side and jQuery at the client side, this book will show you a lot of tricks to help the interaction between the two. This is not a book about Ajax, as it is important that you don't concentrate on the data transfer part of it—instead, we'll concentrate on the jQuery and PHP part of it, and the Ajax part of it will be treated as a simple consequence of what we are doing.

jQuery makes Ajax almost invisible; in fact, it is so simple to use that after a while, you completely forget that what you are doing is something that could not be done easily even just four years ago. This is fantastic, as it allows us to combine the server side with the client side as if they are literally speaking to each other.

To start off, I'll show you a few tricks, which demonstrate how to relieve some more obvious resource wastes.

The examples discussed are the common patterns that you will have seen being used online or in desktop applications.

- Dynamically populated select boxes, where changing one select box changes the options available in the other select box
- Quick deletes, where deleting an object deletes it immediately from the view instead of waiting till a page has been reloaded, helping the site to appear responsive
- Contextual help, where help can be obtained about an object by simply turning help on, and then clicking an icon near the object
- Inline editing, where a table's data can be edited immediately, instead of needing to load a special forms page to edit it

In Chapter 1, *Introduction and Overview*, I described the example directory layout that will be used throughout the book.

To recap, here is the layout that I used while writing the following examples:

```
http://yoursite.xyz/jquery.min.js
http://yoursite.xyz/2-contextual_help/
http://yoursite.xyz/2-dynamic_select_boxes/
http://yoursite.xyz/2-inline_editing/
http://yoursite.xyz/2-quick_deletes/
```

When starting a new example, you should create a new directory. If the book says "create a file, xyz.html", then the file is created in that new directory.

In all the examples of this book, the library files, including jquery.js and all others we use, will be kept in the root of the examples, while the example files will be kept in their own separate directories.

This allows us to write new example files without needing to always download the library files.

Dynamic select boxes

Frequently on the Internet, you would have come across registration forms where selection of certain fields cause the entire page to refresh in order to show you the details specific to that selection.

An example of that would be countries and cities. It's a natural thing for a web developer to want a person to input the country and city with a select box instead of an input box. This is because cities and countries rarely change, and you really don't want your users making up countries or cities!

However, there are many thousands of cities when you consider the number of countries in the world, and to print them all in a simple registration form is extremely impractical, not to mention their sheer number, as we will see in a later chapter!

Earlier the developers would have come up with a solution like: to add an event watcher, wait for the **Country** select box to be changed, and when this happened, the entire "state" of the form would be sent to the server and a new page would be generated with the country-specific details added.

Country -- please choose -- ⌄
Cities please choose a country first

This was a good solution in those times, but these days, we have the luxury of Ajax.

jQuery allows us to very easily check for the country being selected, and replace the **Cities** select box when the event is triggered. And, the trick to that is so simple, that it's our first example.

Country Ireland ⌄
Cities Cork ⌄

Client-side code

Here's the HTML with the JavaScript embedded in it. I'm going to assume that you've at least used JavaScript before. I'll explain the differences between JavaScript and PHP throughout the book, but the assumption I'm working under is that you're good at PHP, moderate at CSS, and know enough JavaScript to follow along.

In the root of your test web server, place your `jquery.min.js` file, create a directory, `/2-dynamic_select_boxes`, and then place the following HTML in it in a file named `index.html`:

```html
<html>
  <head>
    <script src="/jquery.min.js"></script>
    <script>
      function setup_country_change(){
        // If #country is changed, then call update_cities()
        $('#country').change(update_cities);
      }
      function update_cities(){
        var country=$('#country').attr('value');
        // Call get_cities.php and when retrieved,
        //    call show_cities() with the result.
        $.get('get_cities.php?country='+country, show_cities);
      }
      function show_cities(res){
        // Replace contents of #cities with retrieved result
        $('#cities').html(res);
      }
      // Run setup_country_change() when the document is ready
      $(document).ready(setup_country_change);
    </script>
  </head>
  <body>
    <form>
      <table>
        <tr>
          <th>Country</th>
          <td>
            <select name="country" id="country">
              <option value=""> -- please choose -- </option>
              <option value="ie">Ireland</option>
              <option value="uk">Great Britain</option>
            </select>
```

```
        </td>
      </tr>
      <tr>
        <th>cities</th>
        <td id="cities">please choose a country first</td>
      </tr>
    </table>
  </form>
  </body>
</html>
```

The HTML here is very easy to explain. There is simply a select box for the country, with both the name and the id as `country`, and there is a placeholder table cell with the ID `cities`.

The real magic happens with the JavaScript.

How it works

The main function in jQuery is called `jQuery`. But most people use the common alias `$` as it is already set up with the script and is much shorter.

In PHP, the `$` symbol indicates that the following string is a variable name, but in JavaScript, `$` has no special meaning—it is just another character, which can be used in a variable name. In jQuery's case, `$` is an object. Objects and functions are interchangeable in JavaScript. This means that you can call it using parameters like a function, and it will return a value in the form of a jQuery object instance. You can also use it as a static object and call its methods directly.

To start the book, everything will be explained line by line. As the book progresses, less and less will need to be explained, as you will become familiar with how jQuery works.

```
  $(document).ready(setup_country_change);
```

This line tells the browser to run the `setup_country_change` function when the document (the main structural element in a web page) is ready for manipulation.

This is a very common pattern, and it is found in most jQuery-powered applications. Almost all jQuery scripts start with a request where jQuery calls a specified function when it is ready to start manipulating the document.

Note that in this case, jQuery is being called as a function, but is then further acted upon as an object. The `.` character in JavaScript is almost the same as `->` in PHP, and indicates either a method or an object variable.

So, to paraphrase the whole discussion, the jQuery function is called with the page document as a parameter. jQuery returns an instance of itself as an object, which is then used to call the `ready` method with the function reference, `setup_country_change`.

```
function setup_country_change(){
    $('#country').change(update_cities);
}
```

This is the function that is called when the document is ready to be manipulated. Note that in PHP, there is no concept of "when"—either things happen now, or don't happen at all. In PHP, things always happen in a straightforward manner—you call a function, and the next line is not processed until that function returns a value.

However, JavaScript is a bit more threaded than that—you can have a process running, which might not return a value for a few seconds; so, sometimes, things happen asynchronously.

This can be quite a leap for a straight PHP developer, so please re-read anything you're not sure of.

When the `setup_country_change` function is called, jQuery is called with the parameter #country. This parameter is a CSS selector, which indicates an element with the ID `country`. The `change` method tells jQuery to set a watch for when the element's value is changed, and when that happens, the `update_cities` function is to be called.

jQuery is usually called with a parameter. The parameter tells jQuery what it has to act on. The parameter can take many forms. In our examples so far, the form has been a CSS selector; in which case, jQuery is told to perform the following action on all the elements that match that selector. It's important to note that this might be more than one object. For example, `$('*')` will match every element in your document. Even if there is just one element in question, internally, jQuery will still be thinking in terms of an array.

```
function update_cities(){
    var country=$('#country').attr('value');
    $.get('get_cities.php?country='+country, show_cities);
}
```

Here's where it gets interesting.

The first line grabs the value of the **Country** select box. Note that `.attr` returns the value of the first element, even if more than one is matched.

And `$.get` is an Ajax call. It tells the client to request data from the server using the first parameter as a URL, and send everything that's returned to the function referenced in the second parameter. The expected data does not need to be in any particular format. In this example, we will expect HTML to be returned by the server.

In PHP, string concatenation is done with the `.` operator. In JavaScript, it's with +.

```
function show_cities(res){
  $('#cities').html(res);
}
```

When the server has done its job and echoed out its result for the requested URL, this function then simply pastes the result directly into the selected element as HTML.

Server-side code

We've looked in-depth into the client-side code. You can see from the jQuery for the **Country** select box that a server-side script needs to be provided, which will read a GET variable for the country and return some HTML, which can then be pasted into the form to complete it.

Here is some example PHP, which will return a select box for Ireland and the UK. Feel free to expand for other countries!

The following code should be saved in a separate file in the same directory as your HTML file. Call this one `get_cities.php`.

```
<?php
switch($_REQUEST['country']){
  case 'ie': // { ireland
    $cities=array(
      'Cork', 'Dublin', 'Galway', 'Limerick',
      'Waterford'
    );
    break;
  // }
  case 'uk': // { United Kingdom
    $cities=array(
      'Bath', 'Birmingham', 'Bradford',
      'Brighton &amp; Hove', 'Bristol',
      'Cambridge', 'Canterbury', 'Carlisle',
      'Chester', 'Chichester', 'Coventry',
      'Derby', 'Durham', 'Ely', 'Exeter',
      'Gloucester', 'Hereford', 'Kingston upon Hull',
      /* and on and on! */
```

```
        'Newport', 'St David\'s', 'Swansea'
      );
    break;
  // }
  default: // { else
    $cities=false;
  // }
}
if(!$cities)echo 'please choose a country first';
else echo '<select name="city"><option>',
 join('</option><option>',$cities),
 '</select>';
?>
```

This code looks at the value of $_REQUEST['country'] and returns HTML based on what was requested.

The last three lines show that the returned HTML is a select box. To re-iterate what the demo shows, a select box is provided by the initial HTML, and when it is changed, jQuery sends a message to the PHP, which provides a new select box that jQuery then grafts into the HTML.

Simple, and elegant.

It is worth mentioning that the code that is returned is just HTML. jQuery cannot tell anything from it other than that it is HTML. It would be more useful if the PHP returned the HTML and a status of success or failure, encapsulated in an object or array, and that is what we will do in the next example.

Quick deletes

Traditionally, web applications worked by sending an entire generated page of HTML to the user, waiting for the user to perform some action, such as a click, and replying with another entire generated page of HTML.

If all that you wanted to do was to delete a single row in a table of hundreds, then it does not make sense to spend time regenerating the hundreds of other rows (database strain), importing and parsing your web templates all over again (hard drive, CPU, and RAM strain), and asking the client to download external resources, such as ads (bandwidth, network lag), all so that you can delete a measly hundred bytes.

The blogging software WordPress is an example of how it should be done. In the control panel for WordPress, whenever a comment is marked as spam or deleted, the comment simply vanishes from the page. The page does not reload.

Unfortunately, most software applications out there are written with just PHP and HTML, and the smallest amount of client-side JavaScript. Those projects are missing out on "wow"ing their users.

To demonstrate quick deletes, consider a list of subscribers to a list in your content management system, as shown in the following screenshot.

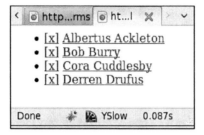

Suppose you want to remove **Cora Cuddlesby** from the list. This is accomplished by clicking the **[x]** link. Ideally, all that should visually happen is that the **Cora Cuddlesby** row should vanish.

Using PHP, you would create the list of subscribers, with a link to a deletion page on the **[x]**, and a link to a subscriber profile page on the subscriber name.

Client-side code

Create an HTML file and save it as `index.html` in a new directory, `/2-quick_deletes` for example. The rest of the files for this example will go in the same directory. In the `<body>` of the document, place the following HTML code (the result of your generated list of subscribers):

```html
<html>
  <head></head>
  <body>
    <ul id="subscribers">
      <li>
        <a href="delete.php?id=3">[x]</a>
        <a href="user.php?id=3">Albertus Ackleton</a>
      </li>
      <li>
        <a href="delete.php?id=6">[x]</a>
        <a href="user.php?id=6">Bob Burry</a>
      </li>
      <li>
        <a href="delete.php?id=2">[x]</a>
```

```
      <a href="user.php?id=2">Cora Cuddlesby</a>
   </li>
   <li>
     <a href="delete.php?id=5">[x]</a>
     <a href="user.php?id=5">Derren Drufus</a>
   </li>
  </ul>
 </body>
</html>
```

In the old "web 1.0" fashion, you would then create a delete script, which verifies that you did want to delete that subscriber, then redirects you back after performing the deletion.

That's a round trip that we want to avoid. It takes too long, and involves loading web pages three times, where we should need do it only once.

This is solved by using some Ajax. We want to click on the **[x]** link, have an "Are you sure?" pop-up message to verify that you clicked the right link, then remove the row directly, without loading a new page.

jQuery is used to replace the **[x]** links with an Ajax call, which sends the deletion request, and removes the `<li>` if it was successful.

Place the following code in the `<head>` section of the above HTML:

```
<script src="/jquery.min.js"></script>
<script>
  function subscribers_init(){
    // If an 'x' link is clicked, run delete_subscriber()
    $('#subscribers li a:first-child')
       .click(delete_subscriber);
  }

  function delete_subscriber(){
    var id=this.href.replace(/.*=/,'');
    this.id='delete_link_'+id;
    if(confirm(
      'Are you sure you want to delete this subscriber?'
    ))
    $.getJSON(
      'delete.php?ajax=true&id='+id,
      remove_row
    );
    return false;
  }
```

```
function remove_row(data){
  if(!data.success)return alert(data.error);
  $('#delete_link_'+data.id)
    .closest('li')
    .remove();
}
$(document).ready(subscribers_init);
</script>
```

In the first line, we link to the jQuery library.

 Again, by default, jQuery is called with $ or the jQuery function (whichever you prefer). In PHP, that would not make sense, as the $ symbol indicates that a variable is being named. However, in JavaScript, $ is just one of the symbols that can be used as part of the actual name of a variable or function, along with the usual letters, numbers, and so on.

Then, the document is told that when it is ready to be manipulated, it should find the first link of each list row in the "subscribers" list, and add an event to each of those so that when it is clicked, the delete_subscriber function is called.

In delete_subscriber, an ID is assigned to the link, then the $.getJSON function is used to send the subscribers' ID to the server. remove_row is set as the callback function — when the PHP script returns its result, it will be sent as a parameter to remove_row. Then, the return false statement tells the browser not to carry on with the normal HTML link, that is, don't follow the link if the called action returned false.

The callback in this example is sent a JavaScript object, which was generated on the server and sent to the client using JSON.

```
if(!data.success)return alert(data.error);
```

Here, if the callback result is false, we inform the user of the reported error with an alert box and exit the function.

Otherwise, we use the link's ID to find its closest parent <li> element and remove it, using the following lines of code:

```
$('#delete_link_'+data.id)
  .closest('li')
  .remove();
```

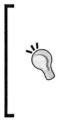

> `$('#delete_link_'+data.id).closest('li').remove();` is an example of **chaining**, where multiple operations are performed on the same object, one after the other.
>
> In PHP, this can be done with objects, if each method call returns a reference to the object itself.
>
> Chaining is a very powerful method and can result in very compact code.

The effect of this is that the row disappears, and we can be sure that the server did its job and removed it there.

Server-side code

On the server side, you need to create a script that deletes the subscriber, then returns a verification that the deletion happened.

Here is a sample PHP script, which will return a JSON "yes" message if the subscriber ID is odd, and "no" if the ID is even. You can use it to test the following script—save it as `delete.php`.

```
<?php
$id=(int)$_REQUEST['id'];
echo ( !($id%2) )?
  "{'id':$id,'success':1}":
  "{'id':$id,'success':0,'error':'Could not delete subscriber'}";
?>
```

To re-iterate (this is important), there are parts of that JavaScript that you may not have seen before as a PHP developer. The most obvious being the asynchronous nature of `.ready` and `.getJSON`. In PHP, when you call a function, it is called synchronously, meaning that the script will not carry on to the next line until a result has been returned.

In JavaScript, event and Ajax calls are usually asynchronous, meaning that you call the function, then carry on with the rest of the script. The result will be returned to a callback function, which is disconnected from the original context—it could be called at any time, and will most likely not remember where the original call came from.

Advanced JavaScript writers can use "closures" to remember the context of the call, but that will not be discussed in the first few chapters of the book. At the time of writing, closures don't exist in PHP, although I've seen references to it for 5.3 and up. Closures will be described later in the book, as they are extremely useful.

For simplicity's sake, when writing events and Ajax, you need to remind the callback function what it was supposed to be working on. In the aforementioned case, the PHP script deleted the subscriber, then returned some JSON, which doesn't just say "The deletion worked", but "The deletion of subscriber $id worked", thus telling the callback function what it should remove from the page.

Contextual help

In some desktop application, there are contextual help applications, where you would click on a help icon, and then click the item you want help on.

It is called "contextual" help because the help that is shown is very specific to the item you need help on, as opposed to the general help, which documents the entire page.

As developers, we like to write concise code. So, when asking for an email address, we might simply write this HTML:

```
<tr><th>Mobile</th><td><input name="mobile" /></td></tr>
```

However, help text tends to be much larger. Obviously, if you don't understand immediately what is required, then it needs to be explained in-depth.

If we were to embed the help text into the HTML source for every element in the page that we intend to use contextual help on, then the resulting text would be probably larger than the page source itself.

This is a waste of bandwidth if the user doesn't require help or needs help on only one item.

It's also a waste of database queries if the text is obtained from a database.

Because of this, it makes sense that contextual help should be downloaded only as required, through Ajax.

The behavior of the contextual help is important—it must be intuitive and unobtrusive.

The example I've written, as can be seen in the following screenshot, starts by
showing a **?** on the top right of the screen:

When clicked on this **?** icon, smaller help icons will be shown next to all the elements
in the page. These icons have help associated with them. When the first icon is
clicked again, the smaller icons will vanish. Clicking the smaller icons will trigger the
Ajax call.

An Ajax call is sent to the help provider application, with the name of the help to be
obtained. A JSON object is returned to jQuery, which then displays the result below
the item that was questioned. The document body is asked to remove the obtained
help from the screen the next time the screen is clicked.

Here's the HTML we will work from. Save it as `contextual_help.html` in your
example directory:

```
<html>
  <head>
    <script src="jquery.min.js"></script>
    <script src="contextual_help.js"></script>
    <style type="text/css">

      #ch_opener{
        position:absolute;top:0;right:0;
        border:1px solid #000;background:#ff0;
        -moz-border-radius:10px;width:20px;height:20px;
        text-align:center;
      }

      .contextual_help_links{
        border:1px solid #000;background:#ff0;
        -moz-border-radius:5px;width:10px;height:10px;
        text-align:center;font-size:8px;display:inline-block;
      }
```

```
    .contextual_help_result{
      position:absolute;border:1px solid #000;
      background:#fff;opacity:.7;
    }
  </style>
</head>
<body>
  <form>
    <table>
      <tr>
        <th>Name</th>
        <td class="contextual_help name">
          <input name="name" />
        </td>
      </tr>
      <tr>
        <th>Email</th>
        <td class="contextual_help email">
          <input name="email" />
        </td>
      </tr>
    </table>
  </form>
</body>
</html>
```

Note the classes added to the table cells. This tells the jQuery script what help text is associated with the cell. The first part, contextual_help, says "there is contextual help associated with this element." The jQuery script sees that, and then takes the string after that to be the name of the help that is requested.

In this example, I've removed the JavaScript from the body of the HTML and placed it externally. Some of the reasons for including JavaScript from an external file are as follows:

- The client will cache the script, reducing bandwidth.
- Easier to read — you won't have to mentally shift between PHP, HTML, JavaScript, and CSS if each language is kept separate.
- Easier to debug.
- Less bandwidth wasted if the JavaScript is not loaded in the first place (search engines) or if JavaScript is loaded on demand, instead of all being loaded at once.
- Neater. In my opinion, neatness is very important as it makes code easier to edit even a year later when you come back to it.

On the server side, it is assumed that a parameter named "name" will be sent, and a JSON object will be returned based on that.

Save the following file as contextual_help.php:

```php
<?php

$name=$_REQUEST['name'];
switch($name){
  case 'email': // {
    $help='Enter your email address here.<br />Please note that it
         will be verified, so make sure it is correct.';
    break;
  // }
  case 'name': // {
    $help='Enter your full name here. No more than 255 letters,
         please!';
    break;
  // }
  default: // {
    $help='Unknown help requested: '.$name;
  // }
}

echo '{"name":"'.addslashes($name).'","help":"'.addslashes($help).'"}';
?>
```

You could enhance that in various ways, as mentioned earlier—make it read from a database, add a multi-lingual element to it, and so on.

Here is the JavaScript that does all the magic; place it in contextual_help.js:

```javascript
function contextual_help_setup(){
  $('<a id="ch_opener" href="javascript:;">?</a>')
    .click(contextual_help_toggle)
    .appendTo(document.body);
}

function contextual_help_toggle(){
  if(document.contextual_help_active){
    $('.contextual_help_links').remove();
    document.contextual_help_active=false;
    return;
  }
  $('<a href="javascript:;" class="contextual_help_links">?</a>')
    .click(contextual_help_call)
```

```
      .appendTo($('.contextual_help'));
    document.contextual_help_active=true;
  }

  function contextual_help_call(){
    var parent_class=this.parentNode.className;
    var help_to_get=parent_class
      .replace(/contextual_help ([^ ]*)( |$)/,'$1');
    $.getJSON(
      'contextual_help.php?name='+help_to_get,
      contextual_help_show
    );
  }

  function contextual_help_show(data){
    var parent_el=$('.'+data.name);
    if(!parent_el.length)return;
    var pos=parent_el.position();
    var style='left:'+pos.left+'px;top:'
      +(pos.top+parent_el.height())+'px;';
    $('<div class="contextual_help_result" style="'+style+'">'
      +data.help+'</div>').appendTo(parent_el);
    contextual_help_toggle();
    $(document.body).click(contextual_help_hide);
  }

  function contextual_help_hide(){
    $(document.body).unbind('click',contextual_help_hide);
    $('.contextual_help_result').remove();
  }
  $(document).ready(contextual_help_setup);
```

See the example in action now by opening `contextual_help.html`.

First, the script is set up unobtrusively with the `contextual_help_setup` function, which adds the **?** icon to the top right of the document.

When that icon is clicked, the `contextual_help_toggle` function either shows, or hides the smaller icons next to their contexts. Each call to this function will alternate (or toggle) the behavior.

If a smaller icon is clicked, then the `contextual_help_call` function determines what help is actually required, by looking at the class name of the element that help is requested from. Then a request is sent to the server.

The server returns the answer to `contextual_help_show`, which shows the result and tells the document to hide the result when it is clicked (with `contextual_help_hide`).

This could be enhanced further, by building up a widget to display the help, which could ask the reader to enhance the help, rate the help, and so on.

Inline editing

Another useful design pattern that is easy to implement is to allow the user to click a piece of text, have it converted to a text input box, and save its updated value on the server.

This is very useful when you have a table of information and want to edit one field in one of the rows. Instead of loading a whole new page to just edit that row, you can edit the data inline and have it saved by the server. This is demonstrated in the following screenshot:

Client-side code

For this example, I've created a table of names and email addresses, to be saved in a new directory, `/2-inline_editing`, as the `inline-editing.html` file. Create a standard HTML page, including the `<html>`, `<head>`, and `<body>` elements. I've provided a sample row below, and you should add a few more yourself.

```
<table>
...
  <tr>
    <td>Bob Burry</td>
    <td>bob.burry@xyzrentals.com</td>
    <td><a href="edit.php?id=6">edit</a></td>
  </tr>
...
</table>
```

In the head section, include the jQuery library as usual, and also include the code for the example as follows:

```
<head>
  <script src="../jquery.min.js"></script>
  <script src="inline_editing.js"></script>
</head>
```

The example HTML will need to be edited to make it easier for jQuery to work with. Edit your table of subscribers like this:

```
<table id="subscribers">
...
  <tr id="subscriber_6">
    <td class="name">Bob Burry</td>
    <td class="email">bob.burry@xyzrentals.com</td>
    <td class="edit"><a href="edit.php?id=6">edit</a></td>
  </tr>
...
</table>
```

All that's needed is to add a few IDs (for unique elements) and classes (for non-unique elements) so that simple jQuery could be written.

The edit link is useless if the user will be able to edit inline. It is included here to show a method known as "progressive enhancement", where an application is written first with the assumption that the browser client does not have JavaScript installed or enabled, and it is then enhanced by adding JavaScript on top of the page, which makes it easier for more modern browsers to work with it.

I have an opinion on JavaScript in the browser that I should mention here—administrators, who will be editing the page contents, can be expected to have JavaScript turned on. After all, there is no point in having a tool if you are not using it, and JavaScript in the admin area (the administrative or backend part of your site) is there to make the administrator's job easier.

On the frontend, though, you cannot expect all readers to have JavaScript enabled. Clients may read with JavaScript turned off for a variety of reasons, or may simply not have JavaScript installed in the first place.

In other words, in a closed environment such as an admin area, you can assume that the user has JavaScript enabled, but on the front-facing part of the website, you should "progressively enhance" your pages, by first writing as if there is no JavaScript, and then adding it afterwards.

Here's the jQuery script, which you should save in an external file named `inline-editing.js`:

```javascript
function inline_editing_init(){
  $('#subscribers .edit').remove();
  $('#subscribers .name,#subscribers .email')
    .click(inline_editing_edit);
}
function inline_editing_edit(){
  if(this.in_edit)return;
  this.in_edit=true;
  var str=$(this).html();
  var w=$(this).innerWidth();
  $(this).empty();
  $('<input>')
    .attr('value',str)
    .blur(inline_editing_save)
    .keypress(inline_editing_key_pressed)
    .css('width',w)
    .appendTo(this)
    .focus();
}
function inline_editing_save(){
  var id,field_name,p;
  p=this.parentNode;
  if(p.originalHTML==this.value)
    return inline_editing_restore(p);
  field_name=p.className;
  id=$(this).closest('tr')[0].id.replace(/.*_/,'');
  $.getJSON(
    'ajax_inline-editing.php',
    {'id':id,'field_name':field_name,'value':this.value},
    inline_editing_callback
  );
}
function inline_editing_key_pressed(e){
  if(!e.which)inline_editing_restore(this.parentNode);
}
function inline_editing_restore(el){
  $(el).html(el.originalHTML);
  el.in_edit=false;
}
function inline_editing_callback(data){
```

```
    var el=$('#subscriber_'+data.id+' .'+data.field_name)[0];
    if(!data.success){
      inline_editing_restore(el);
      return alert(data.error);
    }
    $(el)
      .empty()
      .text(data.value);
    el.in_edit=false;
  }
$ (document).ready(inline_editing_init);
```

This is quite a bit more complex than the previous examples, but when broken down function by function, it should make sense.

- `inline_editing_init`: This function is used to remove the edit links, and add an event to all names and emails so that the `inline_editing_edit` function is called if they are clicked.

- `inline_editing_edit`: This function is used to convert the table cell into an input box so that it can be edited. It will save the original value. If a key is pressed, it will call the `inline_editing_key_pressed` function. If the input box is "blurred" (when you click outside the box or change its focus), it will call the `inline_editing_save` function.

- `inline_editing_save`: This function will restore the table cell and exit, if the value of the field has not changed. Otherwise, it will get the ID of the subscriber from the parent `<tr>` element, the field name from the `<td>` class, and submit all of that along with the new value through Ajax to `ajax_inline-editing.php`, with `inline_editing_callback` as the callback function.

- `inline_editing_key_pressed`: This function will be used if the user presses the *Esc* key. It will simply restore the table cell to its original value.

- `inline_editing_restore`: This is the function that handles the restoring.

- `inline_editing_callback`: This function will update the table cell with the new value if the server-side save was successful. Otherwise, it will restore the table cell with the original value.

The preceding jQuery script is a bit more complicated than the previous one. You should have no problem understanding each function in itself.

This example shows the jQuery $ object being called in quite a few ways. Some of them have been seen in the chapter already, but I'll describe them all again here, as it's the first example to use them all at the same time.

- `$('#subscribers .edit')`: This tells jQuery to run the following method on any elements, which match that CSS. This can be extremely powerful. jQuery has its own internal CSS selector engine, which at the time of writing, is more standards-compliant than every browser's internal engine. You should feel free to use any CSS selector knowledge you have.

- `$(el)` and `$(this)`: These are examples of jQuery being run on specified elements. In this case, `el` is a variable, and `this` is like the `$this` variable in PHP's OOP.

- `$('<input>')`: In this case, jQuery actually creates the element that it is supposed to run on.

- `$.getJSON`: This is an example of jQuery being run with no particular target in mind. You can think of this as similar to calling a static function in a class. In JavaScript, functions and classes are basically the same. Functions can contain subfunctions.

Most functions in $ return an instance of $, which can be used to run further functions on. For example, `$(el).empty().text(data.value);` empties the `el` element, and then fills it with text from `data.value`. This is called **chaining**. An equivalent in PHP might be:

```
new jQuery($css_selector)->empty()->text($data->value);
```

It can sometimes be confusing to read a script and see $ used in some places and not in others. For example, we have the line `$(el).html(el.originalHTML);` followed immediately by `el.in_edit=false;`. The shortest way to explain this is that if a jQuery function is to be called, use $; and if a variable is to be set directly on an element, apply it directly.

$ usually returns a $ instance, but in some cases, you will want the actual element being worked on. In this case, you can treat the $ as an array — $ (*selector*) `[0]` will return the element being worked on, and $ (*selector*) `[1]` and up will return any others if there are multiple elements being worked on.

Server-side code

As before, I'll supply a sample of PHP. This one again returns success if the subscriber's ID is even and failure if it's odd. Save it as `ajax_inline-editing.php`.

```php
<?php
$id=(int)$_REQUEST['id'];
$field_name=addslashes($_REQUEST['field_name']);
$value=addslashes($_REQUEST['value']);
echo ( !($id%2) )?
  "{'id':$id, 'field_name':'$field_name', 'success':1,
                                         'value':'$value'}":
  "{'id':$id, 'field_name':'$field_name', 'success':0, 'error':
                                         'Could not save data'}";
?>
```

Summary

In this chapter, we looked at a few quick examples of how to interface PHP and jQuery.

The examples we looked at included:

- **Dynamic select boxes**: Change the contents of the second select box based on the choice made in the first.
- **Quick deletes**: Delete an object from the page without reloading the entire page.
- **Contextual help**: Apply contextual help to specific objects on the page.
- **Inline editing**: Convert a table into an on-the-fly editor for its table cells.

In the next chapter, we will look at jQuery tabs and accordions, and how to have PHP manage them for you.

3
Tabs and Accordions

A **tab** is a way of separating content, yet keeping it easy to flick from one piece to another, similar to the labels in a binder.

In a web browser's main application, the tabbed areas are completely separate web pages. In a web page, though, the information is usually related, for example various pages of a form.

An **accordion** is similar to a tab. It separates parts of related data so that only one piece of data is visible at a time. Throughout the chapter, when I speak about tabs, the same information can usually be applied to accordions as well.

The main visual difference between the two is that, with tabs, the handles for flicking between the various pages of data are kept either horizontally or vertically along an edge of the tabbed area. However, with accordions, the handles are more akin to chapter headings, as they are shown interleaved with the pages.

Another visual difference is that with a tab, the tabbed area immediately shifts to the newly selected area, but with an accordion, the shift is shown as an animation—the old page slides closed as the new page slides open.

Accordions are similar to "code folding" in an IDE, in which you open only the part of the data that you're interested in reading, and the rest stays closed until you need it. This makes it very easy to find the piece of data or text that you were looking for, without wading through the rest.

Implementation-wise, the two are similar—you need to display the data, place markers to indicate the page/tab changes, and then run a script to make it all work.

In this chapter, we will have a look at the following points:

- Creating tabs and accordions using jQuery and jQuery UI
- Managing tabs and accordions using a rich text editor and a bit of PHP
- Using Ajax to populate your accordion and tab panels

Using a jQuery tab plugin

The jQuery website has a whole load of plugins available at `http://plugins.jquery.com/`, and some of the cream of the crop are selected to become part of the UI project, available at `http://jqueryui.com/`. This project covers all the common needs of web developers, using a neatly integrated suite of widgets.

> jQuery UI is a separate project from the main jQuery library. The aim of jQuery UI is to provide a set of the most commonly needed widgets, with good-looking CSS themes to support them.
>
> We will use jQuery UI extensively in this book because when starting out with jQuery, what you want to do might have already been done superbly by the jQuery UI team.
>
> jQuery UI is hosted at `http://jqueryui.com/`, and has some of the same developers as the main jQuery library.

Tabs are available for most of the visual programming languages, and the method used to generate them is very common.

In the screenshot here, you can see that a tab widget is composed of two main sections, all enclosed in a containing wrapper:

- **Tabs List**
- **Tabs Content**

The **Tabs List**, which has a number of clickable tab labels, can go on any of the four sides of the **Tabs Content** panel (or could even be completely separate if you want!). However, the most common configuration you'll see will be with the labels near the top.

When a label in the tabs list is pressed, the page (or page section) visible in the main panel is replaced with the newly selected tab's page. This page can either be already hardcoded into the HTML of the document, or can be loaded dynamically through Ajax from the server.

To start with, we'll use hardcoded tabs.

Client-side code

Client-side code needs two new external files, listed as follows:

- The main JavaScript file for the jQuery UI project, available at http://ajax. googleapis.com/ajax/libs/jqueryui/1.7.2/jquery-ui.min.js
- A sample CSS file for that project, available at http://ajax.googleapis. com/ajax/libs/jqueryui/1.7.2/themes/ui-lightness/jquery-ui.css

Download these files and place them in the directory above the examples (where you already have the jquery.min.js file).

A quick reminder—if your demo directory is http://examples/phpandjquery/, then the jquery.min.js and other library files should go in that directory, and your demo files should go in a directory under it, such as http://examples/ phpandjquery/tabs/.

Now, in your example directory, create a file named tabs.html and put the following content into it:

```
<html>
  <head>
    <script src="../jquery.min.js"></script>
    <script src="../jquery-ui.min.js"></script>
    <script>
      $(document).ready(function() {
      $("#tabs").tabs();
```

```
        });
      </script>
      <link rel="stylesheet" type="text/css" href="../jquery-ui.css" />
    </head>
    <body>
      <div id="tabs">
        <ul>
          <li><a href="#tabs-1">Nunc tincidunt</a></li>
          <li><a href="#tabs-2">Proin dolor</a></li>
          <li><a href="#tabs-3">Aenean lacinia</a></li>
        </ul>
        <div id="tabs-1">
          <p>
            Proin elit arcu, rutrum commodo, vehicula tempus,
            commodo a, risus.
          </p>
        </div>
        <div id="tabs-2">
          <p>
            Morbi tincidunt, dui sit amet facilisis feugiat,
            odio metus gravida ante, ut pharetra massa metus id nunc.
          </p>
        </div>
        <div id="tabs-3">
          <p>
            Mauris eleifend est et turpis. Duis id erat.
            Suspendisse potenti.
          </p>
          <p>
            Duis cursus. Maecenas ligula eros, blandit nec,
            pharetra at, semper at, magna. Nullam ac lacus.
            Nulla facilisi.
          </p>
        </div>
      </div>
    </body>
  </html>
```

In this code, you will see that the tabs are defined by creating the navigation row using a `<ul>` block. This is followed by the tab pages themselves, all contained within a wrapper, the tabs `<div>`.

Note that each item in the `<ul>` menu is a link to a tab page defined using `<div>` tags in the section below it. I've highlighted two lines in the code to show how they are connected.

Note the text used in the example: "Lorem Ipsum" text is traditionally used in publishing and graphic design as placeholder text to help demonstrate a layout. The actual text itself is not important, as it is only there to fill out the shape of the layout.

You can generate your own Lorem Ipsum text using the generator at `http://www.lipsum.com/`.

To reiterate, there are three steps for the tabs implementation:

1. A wrapper is created to hold everything together and identify the tabs area. In the previous code, this is the `#tabs` division.

2. A menu is created, which links to each of the tab pages. In the aforementioned code, it is the `<ul>` section.

3. The tabs themselves follow the menu, each described in a `<div>` having an ID, which is linked to a menu item.

Implementing these steps, you'll get:

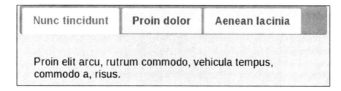

The `$(document).ready` block tells jQuery to apply tabs to the element with the `tabs` ID. You could change that to a class name if you prefer, for example `".tabs"`. Doing so will allow you to have multiple tab widgets on the page. In CSS, there should only be one element of any ID on a page, but you can have as many elements sharing the same class name as you want. But in our example, there is only one tab set, so I chose to use an ID, `#tabs`.

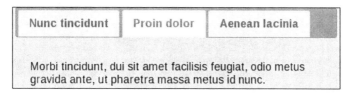

Looking at tabs from a PHP programmer's point of view, it is easy to think that there is something complex about them that makes them work.

However, behind the scenes, there is not much going on.

Instead of converting the block of HTML into some fancy advanced widget as you might imagine, all that happens is that the code is given some class names, which change the various tabs' visibility according to what the reader has clicked on.

Here is an image of our HTML tabs, without the CSS applied:

- Nunc tincidunt
- Proin dolor
- Aenean lacinia

Proin elit arcu, rutrum commodo, vehicula tempus, commodo a, risus.

Morbi tincidunt, dui sit amet facilisis feugiat, odio metus gravida ante, ut pharetra massa metus id nunc.

Mauris eleifend est et turpis. Duis id erat. Suspendisse potenti.

Duis cursus. Maecenas ligula eros, blandit nec, pharetra at, semper at, magna. Nullam ac lacus. Nulla facilisi.

If you remove the `<link>` element in the example, you will see that the code is displayed exactly as you might expect if there was no JavaScript applied at all.

Using a DOM inspection tool, such as Firebug (`http://getfirebug.com/`) for Firefox, Web Inspector for Safari, and so on to inspect the elements, you can see that classes have been added to the elements to allow them to be styled. This is illustrated in the following screenshot:

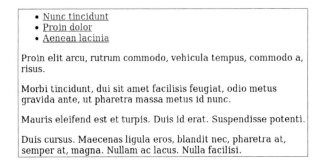

If you plan to create your own styles to handle the tabs, then using Firebug to inspect the added classes is possibly the best way to work on it. You can even edit the CSS on the fly, allowing you to find the look that you want before you commit the actual rules to the stylesheet.

Note that a lot of DOM inspector tools allow you to change the CSS rules "on the fly", but then you need to write those CSS rules into the CSS files to make them permanent.

Server-side considerations

When you are creating a Content Management System (CMS) that is targeted to be used by someone who is not HTML or jQuery literate, it is important that you make it as easy as possible to create tabs or accordions, without requiring that they go and learn HTML.

If the tab is based on an administrator's input (for example, a text area or rich text editor in the CMS's administration area), how do you create the separate tabs – does each tab have its own form or do you somehow manage it with one form? The answer to this is obvious – one form is better than many. But how is that done?

> CMSs have a frontend, where readers can access the main content of your site, and a backend, where an administrator logs in and creates or edits this content.
>
> I use the words "admin area" to indicate the logged-in administration area.
>
> Usually, the admin area is used by a non-technical person, who enters content using forms provided by CMS developers.
>
> When the book says content is created "in the admin area", it means that content is created using a form in the logged-in administrative part of the CMS.

We'll look into methods of doing this later in the chapter. For now, let's look at accordions.

Using jQuery accordion plugins

Accordions are very similar to tabs. They show a single pane of information at a time, and you can navigate through the panes by clicking on a header link for the pane you want to see.

There are some differences between how a jQuery accordion is defined and how a jQuery tab is defined. These implementation differences can be understood by considering how the information should be shown when JavaScript is disabled in the browser – tabs are discrete sections of information (like chapters, maybe), but accordions are usually used only to make the continuous text easier to read.

Again, the jQuery UI project already has a good implementation of accordions built into its core files. So, you don't need to download an extra plugin. But if you wish to use non-standard tricks, such as horizontal accordions (versus vertical, which is the norm), then you should look through `http://plugins.jquery..com/` to decide on what exactly you need.

In tabs, the HTML was arranged such that the tab headers were in a section above the tab content, whereas in accordions, the headers are between the content sections.

Client-side code

Create a new file in your example directory, and call it `accordion.html`. It should contain the following code:

```html
<html>
  <head>
    <script src="../jquery.min.js"></script>
    <script src="../jquery-ui.min.js"></script>
    <script>
      $(document).ready(function() {
        $("#accordion").accordion();
      });
    </script>
    <link rel="stylesheet" type="text/css" href="../jquery-ui.css" />
  </head>
  <body>
    <div id="accordion">
      <h3>Nunc tincidunt</h3>
      <div>
        <p>
          Proin elit arcu, rutrum commodo, vehicula tempus,
          commodo a, risus.
        </p>
      </div>
      <h3>Proin dolor</h3>
      <div>
        <p>
          Morbi tincidunt, dui sit amet facilisis feugiat,
          odio metus gravida ante, ut pharetra massa metus
          id nunc.
        </p>
      </div>
      <h3>Aenean lacinia</h3>
      <div>
```

```
    <p>
       Mauris eleifend est et turpis. Duis id erat.
       Suspendisse potenti.
    </p>
    <p>Duis cursus. Maecenas ligula eros, blandit nec,
       pharetra at, semper at, magna. Nullam ac lacus.
       Nulla facilisi.
    </p>
      </div>
    </div>
  </body>
</html>
```

This code is almost exactly the same as that for tabs. So, it's worth looking at the differences.

The code we just saw was written by copying the code for defining tabs and moving a few lines to match how accordions work. We'll now compare how they both are written.

As already mentioned, in the HTML, the headers appear before the content sections in this case. So, it is essential to make sure that before any jQuery is applied, the content is easy to read and the header locations make sense.

In case of tabs, you needed to supply links to the tab panes, so the navigation section had `href="#..."` links, and the tab content divisions had corresponding IDs. However, in case of accordions, because the headers are directly above the content divisions that they control, there is no need to supply a link to the content—jQuery already knows that the next element to the header is the content it should manage.

Another difference is that you don't need to apply the CSS to see this effect. This is because the accordion is a fairly simple effect and the location of everything is fairly fixed (versus tabs, where the navigation bar might be on the top, at the bottom, and so on). Also, the accordion effect works even without any applied CSS. This can be seen in the following example screenshot, which shows the same content as the previous example screenshot:

Nunc tincidunt

Proin elit arcu, rutrum commodo, vehicula tempus, commodo a, risus.

Proin dolor

Aenean lacinia

The JavaScript for applying the accordion code to the HTML is identical to how the tabs were applied—just tell the `$(document).ready` method to run the `accordion` function on elements that are found using a CSS selector:

```
$(document).ready(function() {
    $("#accordion").accordion();
});
```

One thing for designers to watch out for here is the accordion effect. By default, this has fixed height, and the height is decided by measuring the first content panel. Because of this, you may end up with scroll bars, as can be seen in the example image.

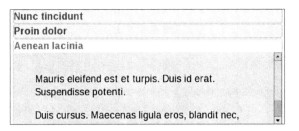

To fix this, change the `.accordion()` call to set `autoHeight` to false:

```
$(document).ready(function() {
 $("#accordion").accordion({
  autoHeight:false
 });
});
```

Doing this will let the content panel open fully.

Server-side management of accordions

This section will show how to create accordions from your content in the admin area of the CMS, without needing to edit class names or build strict HTML structures.

Because of the way jQuery UI expects the accordion markup to appear, alternating header and content sections, it is very simple to manage from a site administrator's point of view.

The average website on the Internet is not managed by a webmaster who is proficient in HTML, JavaScript, PHP, and so on, and that's the way it should be—people like you and me build tools to manage websites so that the average webmaster doesn't have to know the nuts and bolts of it at all.

And this is true of every technology. People driving a car are not expected to know how every part of it works—they just need to know how to steer, speed up, slow down, and so on. To administer a television, you do not need to understand how interlacing works, or what frequencies the channels are received on.

Coming back to the point, the average webmaster no longer needs to know how HTML/CSS/JavaScript/PHP works. They should have a very simple interface to do their job—create stories or pages for their website, with all the fiddly details hidden away and managed by engines that are built by web developers.

The accordion is a good example to show how simplicity can be achieved, because it is very simple already.

Let us imagine that you have a *Pages* section in your CMS, where the admin can create a page by typing into a rich text editor, such as **TinyMCE** (http://tinymce. moxiecode.com/) or **CKeditor** (http://ckeditor.com/, the upcoming successor to FCKeditor).

The administrator (webmaster) knows how to use the editor similarly to a word processor—how to apply bold, italics, headers, and so on. However, he or she is not proficient enough to go into source mode and edit the HTML by hand.

In this case, you cannot expect the administrator to apply the accordion code by hand, so an automated way of doing it must be supplied.

The simplest way to manage this is to check the resulting HTML and if there are any <h3> elements (header 3), then create an accordion from the first <h3> element to the end of the content.

The goal of this section of the chapter is to show simple ways to provide accordions and tabs on the frontend.

While it is possible to extend editors, such as FCKeditor and TinyMCE among others, to display tabs and accordions in the admin area as they are displayed in the frontend, it takes a great deal of effort and very complex programming to achieve this, and also to make sure that your effort does not come undone when a new version of the editor comes out, which is not compatible with your code.

It is much simpler to do this the way I've shown here, and say "All the <h3> elements are headers for accordions."

Client-side code

For this example, you need to download a copy of CKeditor and extract it in the directory above the examples (the same directory for the jQuery and jQuery UI files). I'm using the 3.0b2 version, obtained from the front page of http://ckeditor.com/.

Save the following code as page1.html:

```html
<html>
  <head>
    <script src="../jquery.min.js"></script>
    <script src="../ckeditor/ckeditor.js"></script>
    <script>
    $(document).ready(function(){
      $('textarea.rte').each(function(){
        CKEDITOR.replace(this.name);
      });
    });
    </script>
  </head>
  <body>
    <form action="page2.php" method="post">
      <table width="90%">
        <tr>
          <th style="width:120px">Page Text</th>
          <td>
            <textarea class="rte"
                      style="width:100%;height:200px;"
                      name="body">
            </textarea>
          </td>
        </tr>
```

```
      <tr>
        <th colspan="2"><input type="submit" /></th>
      </tr>
    </table>
  </form>
</body>
</html>
```

This code creates a very simple form, so we can test the accordion generator. Note the usage of jQuery to create the CKeditor instance from all the `<textarea>` elements that have the `rte` class. This is another example of **Unobtrusive JavaScript**.

The unobtrusive method surprisingly is less verbose than if we were to ignore the HTML and write the JavaScript directly.

The resulting form will look like the following:

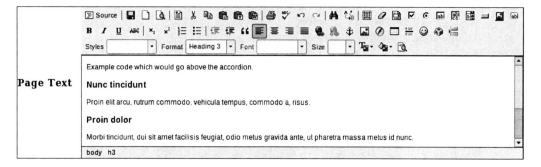

The administrator would enter text into the form in order to have it as a page on the website's frontend. In the above screenshot, the bold text lines are header 3, and we want to convert them into the headers of the accordion.

Server-side code

On the server side, you would normally want to record the form data in a database, so as to call it at some later point. However, before it is shown to the public, you need to modify the code slightly to add the accordion information.

We need to come up with a way to take the HTML generated by the rich text editor, and convert it so that all `<h3>` elements become accordion headers.

We'll now take a look at the code that will demonstrate creation of an accordion from the data entered into the above form.

Just the conversion

Save the following code in a file as `page2.php` in the same directory as `page1.html`:

```php
<?php
$html=@$_REQUEST['body'];
if(strpos($html,'<h3')===false)
$converted=$html;
else{ // accordion found
  // Split the submitted HTML apart at the <h3> elements
  $panels=explode('<h3',$html);
  // Start the accordion. Data before the first <h3> element is
  // prepended to it.
  $converted=array_shift($panels).'<div class="accordion">';

   // Now, loop over each <h3> and add it to the accordion
  foreach($panels as $panel){
    // Break $panel into two pieces:
    // 1. The accordion header.
    // 2. The accordion panel content.

    $panel_bits=explode('</h3>',$panel);
    // header
    $converted.='<h3'.$panel_bits[0].'</h3>';
    // panel content
    $converted.='<div>'.$panel_bits[1].'</div>';
  }
 // Finish the HTML for the accordion
  $converted.='</div>';
}
echo $converted;
?>
```

When the form is submitted, the content will be altered if an `<h3>` element is found (check the source of the results page). At this point, you can either save it in the database, or display it immediately.

You could do the conversion at the point of displaying it to the end reader (expensive), or save both the submitted data and the converted data to separate database fields and print the converted data out to the reader (slightly inefficient). You could also do the conversion and save it to a single database field, discarding what was actually submitted.

The last option, in spite of being the most efficient, is not a good idea. This is because if the data is to be edited again, what you edit will not be the same as what it was before, that is the data you entered into the database the first time. By editing it after conversion has taken place, you risk breaking the data's integrity or any strict HTML formats that had been placed on it.

The two-field method is the best idea. You do the conversion and save both the original and converted versions. The reader is shown the converted version with the accordion added, whereas the administrator, if the page is to be re-edited, is given the original version back. When it's saved again, the data is again converted and saved, like the first time.

Now show the data with the accordions

On the frontend, you must have already displayed this code with the jQuery code in the `<head>` section. Now, remove the `echo $converted` line from the `page2.php` file, and add the following lines after the `?>`:

```html
<html>
  <head>
    <script type="text/javascript" src="../jquery.min.js"></script>
    <script type="text/javascript" src="../jquery-ui.min.js">
    </script>
    <script type="text/javascript">
      $(document).ready(function() {
        $(".accordion").accordion({
          autoHeight:false
        });
      });
    </script>
    <link rel="stylesheet" type="text/css" href="../jquery-ui.css" />
  </head>
  <body>
    <?php echo $converted;?>
  </body>
</html>
```

Now, re-create your alternating header/content example in the form we created earlier and submit the form again.

> Example code which would go above the accordion.
>
> **Nunc tincidunt**
> Proin dolor
>
> > Morbi tincidunt, dui sit amet facilisis feugiat, odio
> > metus gravida ante, ut pharetra massa metus id
> > nunc.
>
> **Aenean lacinia**

This time you'll see that the conversion has worked. Anything with <h3> before it has been converted to an accordion panel.

Note that this is perfect for simple pages, but very complex pages that include tables or multiple accordions would need a more complex solution.

I'll leave that as an exercise for you!

Server-side management of tabs

Tabs are a bit more complex than accordions, because the navigation is separate from the panels themselves.

There are a number of solutions for creating simple administration forms for managing them.

With a little server-side code, we can use exactly the same trick as we did for the accordion, and create tabs from all the content in the page that follows an <h3> element.

For the client-side code, simply copy the client-side code from the accordion demonstration we discussed. The only change will be on the server side.

Server-side code

In this method, the administrator (webmaster) will write normally, that is, with headers followed by content. If an <h3> element is used in the content, the content following it will become a tab.

Just the conversion

The following code will read the submitted HTML and create a `$converted` variable from it, which will contain the tabs-ready version:

```php
<?php
  $html=@$_REQUEST['body'];
  if(strpos($html,'<h3')===false)
    $converted=$html;
  else{ // tab found
    $menu=array();
    $tabs=0;
    $tab_c='';
    // Split the submitted HTML apart at the <h3> elements
    $panels=explode('<h3',$html);

    // Start the tab wrapper. Data before the first <h3>
    // element is prepended to the wrapper.
    $converted=array_shift($panels).'<div class="tabs"><ul>';

    // Loop over each <h3> section to extract tab sections
    foreach($panels as $panel){
      // Break $panel into two pieces:
      // 1. tab name, to be added to the menu <ul>
      // 2. tab content, to be added to the below menu
      $panel_bits=explode('</h3>',$panel);
      $menu[]=preg_replace('/^[^>]*>/','',$panel_bits[0]);
      $tab_c.='<div id="tab-'.($tabs++).'">'.
      $panel_bits[1].'</div>';
    }

    // Create the menu section and add to the tab wrapper
    foreach($menu as $k=>$v)
      $converted.='<li><a href="#tab-'.$k.'">'.$v.'</a></li>';

    // Add the tabs' content panels
    $converted.='</ul>'.$tab_c.'</div>';
  }
  echo $converted;
?>
```

After running this code, you have the converted content in `$converted`. If you examine the converted HTML, you'll see that the `<h3>` elements have been moved to a separate `<ul>` section above the content, and the rest of the code is sectioned into divisions, ready to be acted upon by the tabs plugin.

> Note the usage of `preg_replace` in this code—in rich text editors, it's sometimes incredibly easy for the administrator to accidentally add style information to an element; so, the element is not a pristine `<h3>`, but could be something more like `<h3 style="color:red">`. The `preg_replace` function is needed to work around any possible changes and grab `<h3>` regardless of what might have been done in the admin area.
>
> If you wish to expand on the example, you might also wish to rewrite it using an XML, SGML, or DOM extension, which will allow you to ignore the HTML completely and concentrate on the document structure instead.

Now show the data with the tabs

The tab-encoded HTML is shown in the same way as the accordion-encoded HTML. Simply echo the HTML to the screen, wrapped by the code that handles the plugin.

Again, remove the `echo $converted` line from the conversion code example and add the following lines:

```
<html>
  <head>
    <script type="text/javascript" src="../jquery.min.js"></script>
    <script type="text/javascript"
            src="../jquery-ui.min.js"></script>
    <script type="text/javascript">
    $(document).ready(function() {
      $(".tabs").tabs();
    });
    </script>
    <link rel="stylesheet" type="text/css" href="../jquery-ui.css" />
  </head>
  <body>
    <?php
      echo $converted;
    ?>
  </body>
</html>
```

Now, re-create your HTML in the form we created earlier and submit the form again.

The only thing changed between this and the accordion version is the call, `.tabs()`.

If you change the `.tabs()` line to the following, then the page will display either accordions or tabs, depending on what is provided in the form (you might save some of the admin pages using accordions for `<h3>` elements, and others using tabs).

```
$(document).ready(function() {
  $(".accordion").accordion({
    autoHeight:false
  });
  $(".tabs").tabs();
});
```

Apart from the more complex problems of multiple tabs, multiple accordions, and nested tabs or accordions (which are beyond the scope of this book), the only problem with the examples so far is that they use either tabs or accordions, but never both. That will be solved next.

Using special codes to define tabs

Using an `<h3>` element to define a break in a tab or accordion is fine for simple CMS forms, but it's not very flexible. What if you want to do both?

One solution is to create some text codes for tabs. These codes would be unique to tabs and should not be confused with anything else.

Note that these are custom text codes created by you. They need to be unique to your application, and should not confuse the browser into trying to render them as, say, CSS or HTML.

See the following image for a visual explanation of how the codes will be used:

```
this text will appear above the tabs

{{TABSTART}}

Nunc tincidunt

Proin elit arcu, rutrum commodo, vehicula tempus, commodo a,
risus.

Proin dolor

Morbi tincidunt, dui sit amet facilisis feugiat, odio metus
gravida ante, ut pharetra massa metus id nunc.

{{TABPAGE}}

Aenean lacinia

Mauris eleifend est et turpis. Duis id erat. Suspendisse potenti.

Duis cursus. Maecenas ligula eros, blandit nec, pharetra at,
semper at, magna. Nullam ac lacus. Nulla facilisi.

Nunc a lorem

Pellentesque risus nibh, lacinia nec, eleifend at, congue sed,
lacus.

Lorem ipsum dolor sit amet, consectetur adipiscing elit.

Aliquam tellus nisi, volutpat vel, vestibulum eu, porta et, libero.

{{TABEND}}

this text will appear below the tabs
```

I've included an example above. Notice how the {{TABPAGE}} code is used to indicate a break in the tabs. And on both tab pages, there are `<h3>` elements, so the result we're looking for will be two tab pages with accordions on both.

In our example, we are using the following codes:

- **{{TABSTART}}**: This code indicates where to start tabbing.
- **{{TABPAGE}}**: This code indicates where to "page-break" to the next tab.
- **{{TABEND}}**: This code indicates where to stop tabbing.

The server-side code will parse the submitted data, and use the above codes to build HTML that will display tabs on the frontend.

Using codes this way is useful for a webmaster because he or she can now type directly into the rich text editor without needing to use HTML, and for a PHP developer because it doesn't involve any hacking of the rich text editor to figure out a way to do the same with JavaScript—this can get pretty complex very quickly (as described earlier in the chapter).

The double curly brackets ({{ and }}) are used because in normal usage, it's extremely rare to see them. So, we can be sure that it will not conflict with something the webmaster would normally write.

Client-side code

For the client-side code, again, copy the form created for the accordion demonstration.

In this demonstration, we want to show both accordions and tabs working together. Tabs will be handled using the codes we just discussed, and accordions will be applied to all the <h3> elements.

So, in the form, enter some text that uses them both.

Server-side code

Because the end goal in this case is to provide tabs, which will be used to break a story into various pages, we don't need to extract page titles for those tabs.

Usually, long online stories will be broken into separate pages, each with a title such as "page 1", "page 2", and so on.

Because these are predictable series, we can automate them.

The following code is a combination of tab and accordion conversions from previous examples:

```php
<?php
$html=isset($_REQUEST['body'])?$_REQUEST['body']:' ';
function convert_accordions($html){
  if(strpos($html,'<h3')===false)
    $converted=$html;
  else{ // Accordion found
    $panels=explode('<h3',$html);
    $converted=array_shift($panels).'<div class="accordion">';
    foreach($panels as $panel){
      $panel_bits=explode('</h3>',$panel);
      $converted.='<h3'.$panel_bits[0].'</h3>';     // header
      $converted.='<div>'.$panel_bits[1].'</div>'; // panel content
    }
    $converted.='</div>';
  }
  return $converted;
}
function convert_tabs($html){
  // Add {{TABSTART}}, {{TABEND}} if missing
  if(strpos($html,'{{TABSTART}}')===false)$html='{{TABSTART}}'.$html;
```

```php
    if(strpos($html,'{{TABEND}}')===false)$html=$html.'{{TABEND}}';
    $tabwidgets=explode('{{TABSTART}}',$html);
    // Start by applying accordions to the non-tabs space above
    // the tabs
    $converted=convert_accordions(array_shift($tabwidgets));
    // Convert the rest of the space into tabs
    $tabwidgets_num=0;
    foreach($tabwidgets as $widget){
      $widget_bits=explode('{{TABEND}}',$widget);
      // Extract individual tab pages
      $panels=explode('{{TABPAGE}}',$widget_bits[0]);
      $tabs=1;
      $tab_c='';
      $menu=array();
      foreach($panels as $panel){
        $menu[]='Page '.$tabs;
        $tab_c.='<div id="tab-'.$tabwidgets_num.'-'.($tabs++).'">'
          .convert_accordions($panel)
          .'</div>';
      }
      $converted.='<div class="tabs"><ul>';
      foreach($menu as $k=>$v)
        $converted.='<li><a href="#tab-'.$tabwidgets_num
                   .'-'.($k+1).'">'.$v.'</a></li>';
      $converted.='</ul>'.$tab_c.'</div>'
                 .convert_accordions($widget_bits[1]);
      $tabwidgets_num++;
    }
    return $converted;
}
if(preg_match('/{{TAB(START|END|PAGE)}}/',$html))
  $converted=convert_tabs($html);
else
  $converted=convert_accordions($html);
?>
<html>
  <head>
    <script type="text/javascript" src="../jquery.min.js"></script>
    <script type="text/javascript"
            src="../jquery-ui.min.js">
    </script>
    <script type="text/javascript">
      $(document).ready(function() {
        $(".accordion").accordion({
          autoHeight:false
        });
        $(".tabs").tabs();
      });
    </script>
```

```
    <link rel="stylesheet" type="text/css" href="../jquery-ui.css" />
  </head>
  <body>
    <?php
      echo $converted;
    ?>
  </body>
</html>
```

This example code will actually extract the multiple tabs if you have multiple tabs in the original source. By that, I mean multiple {{TABSTART}}...{{TABPAGE}}... {{TABEND}} sections.

The source code is neatened into functions. Notice how the convert_accordions function is called at a few places throughout the convert_tabs function. This is in case a tab panel contains accordions.

Here's what executing this code will give us:

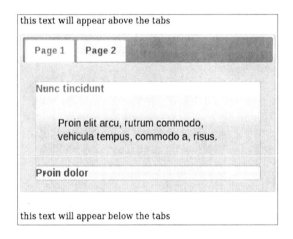

An interesting point to note here is that, if you follow the method described earlier, where two copies of the source are recorded (original and converted), then it does not matter if the conversion process is slow — it only happens once per edit, and the end product will be extremely fast.

So, you should feel free to go through the provided example, and add in as many features as you like, such as HTML optimization, error checking, enhancements, and so on. As an example, you could add a parameter to the {{TABPAGE}} code to indicate the label you want applied to the tab – for example, {{TABPAGE name="configuration"}}. Feel free to write algorithms which might take time to run, because it will not affect the speed of the frontend reader's download.

Loading accordion panels through Ajax

One of the advantages of accordions is that they allow you to read large tracts of text a little at a time.

As a consequence, we don't need to load all of the content as soon as the page is displayed, if it's not immediately required.

We should be able to simply show the available accordion panels, and when an accordion is selected, load its content from the server as the browser expands the panel.

To demonstrate this, I've written an example using a book, *Great Expectations*, by Charles Dickens.

You would most likely not sit down in front of your screen and read the whole book in one sitting. It makes sense that if you are going to read a long piece of text on the screen, it would be broken up into chapters or other sections, and you would choose which one to read.

To try this example out, create a new demo directory and download a book in text format into it. I downloaded my example text file from `http://www.gutenberg.org/etext/1400` (plain text, ISO-8859-1).

This example will show how to extract a single chapter for display at a time. Your own production example might need something entirely different (for example, extracting text from a database), so the exact PHP does not matter. I've provided it just for illustrative purposes. The real interesting part is the jQuery.

Client-side code

Place the following code in a file in the directory and call it book.php:

```
<html>
  <head>
    <script src="../jquery.min.js"></script>
    <script src="../jquery-ui.min.js"></script>
    <script>
      $(document).ready(function(){
        $('#chapters').accordion({
          'active':false,
          'collapsible':true,
          'changestart':function(ev,ui){
            var id=ui.newHeader[0].id;
            var chp=id.replace(/chp/,'');
            $.get('get_chapter.php?chp='+chp,function(res){
              $('#chp'+chp+'-content').html(res);
            });
          }
        });
      });
    </script>
    <style type="text/css">
      @import "../jquery-ui.css";
      h2{text-indent:30px}
    </style>
  </head>
  <body>
    <h1>Great Expectations</h1>
    <div id="chapters">
      <?php
        $book=file_get_contents('1400-8.txt');
        $chapters=preg_match_all('/Chapter /',$book,$arr);
        for($i=1;$i<$chapters+1;++$i){
          echo '<h2 id="chp',$i,'">Chapter ',$i,'</h2>';
          echo '<div id="chp',$i,'-content"';
          if($i==1)echo ' style="height:200px"';
            echo '> </div>';
        }
      ?>
    </div>
  </body>
</html>
```

We have two distinct parts here: the PHP to display the initial list of chapters and the JavaScript to manage the accordion.

The PHP reads the file and extracts the number of chapters. In the example case, this is simply a matter of counting how many times the string **Chapter** is repeated.

In this example, the accordion is applied to the `#chapters` `<div>`, which has an alternating series of the `<h2>` and `<div>` elements in it, which become the accordion headers and panels.

In order to start with all chapters closed, we need to add the following two parameters to the `.accordion()` call.

- `collapsible`: This parameter tells the accordion engine whether the accordion is allowed to have all elements closed on it. It defaults to `false`.

- `active`: This parameter tells the accordion engine what panel to open at the start. If you set it to `false`, it will not open any (if `collapsible` is `true`).

Note that in the PHP, we need to set an ID for each `<h2>` and each `<div>`, so that when a title is clicked, we know what chapter to retrieve from the server, and where in the document to paste the retrieved HTML.

Also, note that we set the height of the first element. The accordion sets its height based on the height of the first panel. As we're starting with no content, we need to artificially set its height.

When a title is clicked, the `changestart` event is fired. Here it is again:

```
'changestart':function(ev,ui){
  var id=ui.newHeader[0].id;
  var chp=id.replace(/chp/,'');
  $.get('get_chapter.php?chp='+chp,function(res){
    $('#chp'+chp+'-content').html(res);
  });
}
```

The `ui` parameter is set by jQuery UI and has a few details about the state of the accordion. The `ui.newHeader` object is a reference to the chapter heading that was just clicked.

With that done, we can now extract the chapter number by stripping `chp` from the element's ID, and then we can use `$.get` to retrieve the chapter's HTML and paste it into the accordion at the appropriate point.

Server-side code

On the server side, we just need to provide a method to extract the chapter and send it back to the accordion.

In our example case, it's a simple text file, so here's a small script that handles it—save this as `get_chapter.php`:

```php
<?php
  $book_url='1400-8.txt';
  $book=file_get_contents($book_url);
  $chapters=explode('Chapter ',$book);
  $to_get=isset($_REQUEST['chp'])?(int)$_REQUEST['chp']:1;
  if(!isset($chapters[$to_get]))
    die("no such chapter");
  $chapter=$chapters[$to_get];
  $chapter=str_replace("\r\n\r\n","</p><p>",$chapter);
  $chapter=preg_replace('/^[^<]*<\/p>/','',$chapter);
  echo $chapter.'</p>';
?>
```

Loading tab panels through Ajax

Reading long extracts of text is not what tabs are designed for; they're more for isolating contextually separate sections of a document from each other.

Having said that, we'll follow the previous example (reading a book through accordions) with the same thing but in the tab format, so that we have a comparison.

Tabs are incredibly easy to set up to use Ajax. As we'll see, it's just a matter of adding the URL to retrieve to the menu link.

Client-side code

To see this example in action, copy the entire previous example to a new directory, and replace the `book.php` file with this:

```html
<html>
  <head>
    <script src="../jquery.min.js"></script>
    <script src="../jquery-ui.min.js"></script>
    <script>
      $(document).ready(function(){
        $('#chapters').tabs();
      });
    </script>
    <style type="text/css">
```

```
        @import "../jquery-ui.css";
        #chapters li{padding-bottom:0 !important}
      </style>
    </head>
    <body>
      <h1>Great Expectations</h1>
      <div id="chapters">
        <ul>
          <?php
            $book=file_get_contents('1400-8.txt');
            $chapters=preg_match_all('/Chapter /',$book,$arr);
            for($i=1;$i<$chapters+1;++$i){
              echo '<li><a href="get_chapter.php?chp=',$i,'">'
                ,$i,'</a></li>';
            }
          ?>
        </ul>
      </div>
    </body>
  </html>
```

You'll note that this example is much shorter than the previous one.

47	48	49	50	51	52	53
54	55	56	57	58	59

He lay in prison very ill, during the whole interval between his committal for trial and the coming round of the Sessions. He had broken two ribs, they had wounded one of his lungs, and he breathed with great pain and difficulty, which increased daily. It was a consequence of his hurt that he spoke so low as to be scarcely audible; therefore he spoke very little. But he was ever ready to listen to me; and it became the first

In this example, we didn't have to create dummy tabs for the Ajax to populate—the tabs plugin does that automatically.

Also, we did not need to manually write an event to get a chapter when the header is clicked. By setting up the menu with links to the appropriate page, that is, writing `get_chapter.php?chp=n`, the tabs engine knows to retrieve it by Ajax.

One final thing to note about Ajax and tabs or accordions, is that if you are using tabs or accordions to make it easier for your readers to fill in forms, beware that using Ajax inappropriately will make some of the form disappear, so the reader will not be submitting a complete form.

Summary

In this chapter, we've walked through how to create tabs and accordions using the jQuery UI project.

Following that, we saw a few different server-side scripts, demonstrating how to easily manage the creation of tabs/accordions without requiring editing of HTML.

And finally, we looked at how to use Ajax to populate accordion and tab panels, and the differences between the methods used to achieve this.

In the next chapter, we will look at form validation and how to use the same PHP configuration to validate on both sides—the server and the client side.

4
Forms and Form Validation

Problems can occur when unfiltered form data is inserted into a database or used to send emails.

SQL injection, for example, is a method where an attacker tries to "hack" the site's database by submitting SQL fragments through your forms in an attempt to have them run as actual SQL on the server.

In email forms, spamming robots sometimes try subverting the email-sending mechanism to send their own spam through your server.

Form validation is used to make sure that the data is sane and will not cause problems. For example, if you validate that what you expect to be an email address actually is an email address, or that SQL is properly escaped before running it, then you will go a long way towards stopping these kinds of hacks.

However, validation is not all about security—sometimes it's as simple as making sure that the reader has properly filled the form and hasn't forgotten to give their own contact details. While server-side validation is essential to ensure that your data is correct and clean, client-side validation can improve the usability, reducing the server load as well as the time spent filling and correcting the form before it can be accepted by the server. On the server side, the data absolutely must be checked and declared safe, but the absence of client-side validation would involve reloading the page a few times until the user gets it right. On the client side, form validation will ensure that the user has everything filled out correctly before submitting it, but without server-side validation, this can be easily abused by hackers.

Implementing both client- and server-side validation may seem a bit inefficient and also programmatically silly (why write the same thing in two separate languages?), but there is a good way to do it—you write your validation rules in PHP, and have the PHP generate the JavaScript, so updating the form only involves changing one piece of code.

To be very clear about this, the validation rules are written by you in PHP and will run on the server side, and the same validation rules are then used to automatically generate JavaScript for running on the client side.

This chapter will discuss how to do that, and also how to solve a few other common form problems.

We will address the following:

- Loading select boxes only when they're needed
- Auto-suggestion
- Form validation
- Validating the server side and client side by the same rules
- Validation of client side data using Ajax

Using the jQuery validation plugin

There are a number of validation plugins available online. The one we will use in this chapter is by Jörn Zaefferer, and is one of the longest-lived of those plugins.

If you want to do anything that someone else might already have done in jQuery, there is probably a plugin already existing for you to download.

Before you reinvent any wheels, always check `http://plugins.jquery.com/` to see if there is something there that will do what you want.

Download the zipped package from `http://bassistance.de/jquery-plugins/ jquery-plugin-validation/` and extract it into the examples root directory. The extracted package will make a directory called `jquery-validation`, containing the plugin and some extra files in case you need further capabilities.

Client-side code

Create a new HTML document, call it `form.html`, and insert the following HTML into the body section. It will create a form for us to work with.

```
<form id="contact_form">
  <table>
    <tr><th>Name</th><td><input name="name" /></td></tr>
    <tr><th>Email</th><td><input name="email" /></td></tr>
    <tr><th>Job Status</th><td><select name="job_status">
      <option value=""> -- please choose -- </option>
```

```
        <option>Unemployed</option>
        <option>Employed</option>
        <option>Retired</option>
    </select></td></tr>
    <tr><th>Comments</th><td>
        <textarea name="comments"></textarea>
    </td></tr>
    <tr><th colspan="2"><input type="submit" /></th></tr>
  </table>
</form>
```

This should create a form like the following:

It is easy to imagine what kind of validation would be required for each of these fields.

- **Name** must at least exist
- **Email** should be in a proper email address form
- **Job Status** should be specified
- **Comments** should be of a reasonable length

With the `validate` plugin, that is very simple to set up. Here is the head section of that document:

```
<head>
  <script src="../jquery.min.js"></script>
  <script src="../jquery-validate/jquery.validate.min.js"></script>
  <script>
    $(document).ready(function(){
      $('#contact_form').validate({
        'rules':{
          'name':'required',
          'email':{
            'required':true,
            'email':true
          },
          'job_status':'required',
          'comments':{
```

```
                    'required':true,
                    'minlength':10
                }
            }
        });
    });
  </script>
</head>
```

If you place this code in the head, save, and reload the browser window, you will see that the form is validated.

The `validate` plugin accepts a number of parameters, including events, groups, and messages among other types. In this chapter, we are concerned with the `rules` object, which you can see highlighted in this example, and we'll describe that as we proceed. For a full list of accepted parameters, and demo code of their usage, please visit `http://docs.jquery.com/Plugins/Validation/validate#options`. Try hitting **Submit Query** without filling anything in:

Name		This field is required.
Email		This field is required.
Job Status	-- please choose -- ∨	This field is required.
Comments		This field is required.
	Submit Query	

The validator is activated from the moment you clicked on **Submit Query**. Up until then, it is assumed that you know what you are doing. However, once you click on the submit button, the validator checks the form, and then sets handles on all the form elements so that they are checked "on the fly" as you edit them.

After the validator is activated, the validator will update the validation status as you type:

Name	kae	
Email	kae#verens.com	Please enter a valid email address.
Job Status	Employed ∨	
Comments	hi!	Please enter at least 10 characters.
	Submit Query	

I'd recommend reading through the plugin's documentation. The `validate` plugin does a lot that is outside the scope of this chapter, and it is worth knowing what else it can do, in case you need it in the future.

Setting up jQuery validation from PHP

Client-side validation is very useful, and saves a lot of time. However, if there is no server-side validation to make sure that the input is correct, then there is no guarantee that the data you collect will be correct.

In this case, PHP is very useful to us to manage the form. When you think of it, the form would be defined in the following three areas:

- In the document's head section as part of the JavaScript
- In the body section in the HTML form
- On the server side when validating and submitting the code

If any one of these was different to the rest, then there would be problems.

The simplest way to solve this is to have a single definition of the form in PHP, from which the HTML and JavaScript should be built.

However, HTML is a layout language, and even the simplest form can be laid out in many different ways. For now, we will combine the PHP and JavaScript. Creating a form builder that builds up forms including their validation rules and their layout is a whole project in itself. This chapter concentrates on the validation rules only.

Server-side code (setup)

First off, we define the form validation rules using a PHP array. Save this as form.libs.php in a new example directory:

```php
<?php
$form_rules=array(
  'name'=>array(
    'required'=>true
  ),
  'email'=>array(
    'required'=>true,
    'email'=>true
  ),
  'job_status'=>array(
    'required'=>true
  ),
  'comments'=>array(
    'required'=>true,
    'minlength'=>10
  )
);
?>
```

You can already see that it is very similar to the JavaScript version from the first example.

To complete the validation, all we need to do is translate this configuration so that it is usable by the `validate` plugin.

As the structure is so similar to the JavaScript version, this just involves converting from PHP into JavaScript using JSON.

Client-side code

Copy the `form.html` file from the previous example into the new directory as `form.php`, and edit the top part of it (up to the body) as follows:

```php
<?php require 'form.libs.php'; ?>
<html>
  <head>
    <script src="../jquery.min.js"></script>
    <script src="../jquery-validate/jquery.validate.min.js"></script>
    <script>
      $(document).ready(function(){
        $('#contact_form').validate({
          'rules': <?php echo json_encode($form_rules); ?>
        });
      });
    </script>
  </head>
```

Isn't that incredibly simple? If you examine the output, you will see that it is virtually identical to the original example, with just the whitespace removed.

> Note that json_encode is a function that is available from PHP 5.2 onwards.
>
> If your server version is lower than that, you should consider asking your provider to upgrade, or download and use jsonwrapper, which provides a json_encode function for older PHP versions from.
> http://www.boutell.com/scripts/jsonwrapper.html

We can use the same PHP array to validate on the server side.

Server-side code

In a proper project, I would recommend using something like the Pear Validate package for server-side validation. In this case, though, I will write something simple, to cut down on the dependencies in the example.

Change the HTML form in `form.php` so that it is pointing to a PHP file named `form.submit.php`:

```
<form id="contact_form" method="post" action="form.submit.php">
```

Create a new file named `form.submit.php`:

```php
<?php
require 'form.libs.php';

function get_errors($form_data,$rules){
  // returns an array of errors
  $errors=array();

  // validate each existing input
  foreach($form_data as $name=>$value){
    if(!isset($rules[$name]))continue;
    $hname=htmlspecialchars($name);
    $rule=$rules[$name];

    // make sure that 'required' values are set
    if(isset($rule['required'])
        && $rule['required'] && !$value)
      $errors[]='Field '.$hname.' is required.';

    // 'minlength' inputs need a minimum length
    if(isset($rule['minlength'])
        && strlen($value)<$rule['minlength'])
      $errors[]=$hname.' should be at least '
        .$rule['minlength'].' characters in length.';

    // verify that 'email' inputs are valid email addresses
    if(isset($rule['email']) && $rule['email']
        && !filter_var($value,FILTER_VALIDATE_EMAIL))
      $errors[]=$hname.' must be an email address.';

    $rules[$name]['found']=true;
  }
  // check for missing inputs
  foreach($rules as $name=>$values){
    if(!isset($values['found']) && isset($values['required']) &&
                                   $values['required'])
      $errors[]='Field '.htmlspecialchars($name).' is required.';
```

```
    }
    // return array of errors (or empty array if all is OK)
    return $errors;
}
$errors=get_errors($_POST,$form_rules);
if(!count($errors)){
    // save the data, or post it, or whatever
    echo 'success';
}
else{
    // errors found
    echo '<strong>Errors found in form:</strong><ul><li>';
    echo join('</li><li>',$errors);
    echo '</li></ul><p>Please go back and correct your errors.</p>';
}
?>
```

To test this code, load up `form.php` and turn off JavaScript in your browser. When the form is submitted with no values, a list of errors will be shown.

The `get_errors` function compares a list of inputs to a list of rules, and returns an array of all points where the inputs differ from the rules.

If the array is empty, then the form is valid. Otherwise, it is invalid and a list of errors should be given to the submitter, as follows:

Errors found in form:

- Field name is required.
- Field email is required.
- email must be an email address.
- Field job_status is required.
- Field comments is required.
- comments should be at least 10 characters in length.

Please go back and correct your errors.

You could adapt this so that the form is re-shown with data filled in and errors shown where appropriate, or you can simply print the errors and suggest that the reader press **Back** on their browser and fill in the incorrect values.

Remote validation

Sometimes you will need to verify that the information entered into a form is unique to the server's database, or some other server-side test that cannot easily be done on the client side.

An example is when you are asking someone for user registration details. The point of a user account is that it is a unique identifier. To be unique, it should have one field that is not shared by any other account. These days, it is very common to use the email address as that field. In the past, a username would have been more common, but there are good reasons why an email address is better.

To set this one up, copy the `form.submit.php` file from the previous example to a new example directory. This file will not need to change much. The rest will be rebuilt.

Server-side code (setup)

Here is the `form.libs.php`, which contains the validation rules for the form. Note the new rule terms, which have been highlighted.

```php
<?php
$form_rules=array(
   'email'=>array(
     'required'=>true,
     'email'=>true,
     'remote'=>'form.check-email.php'
   ),
   'password'=>array(
     'required'=>true
   ),
   'password2'=>array(
     'equalTo'=>'#password'
   )
);
?>
```

The `equalTo` rule checks the value of the field and compares it to the value of another field. Note the #, which makes it a CSS selector for an element with that ID. Be sure to always include the ID in the HTML element.

The `remote` rule tells the `validate` plugin to grab a remote URL through Ajax. It expects the URL to return the "false" or "true" string. The `remote` file is sent the field name and value through GET.

Client-side code

On the client side, the only new part added is a custom error message for the **Email** field. Save this file as `form.php`:

```php
<?php require 'form.libs.php'; ?>
<html>
  <head>
    <script src="../jquery.min.js"></script>
    <script src="../jquery-validate/jquery.validate.min.js"></script>
    <script>
      $(document).ready(function(){
        $('#registration_form').validate({
          'rules': <?php echo json_encode($form_rules); ?>,
          'messages': {
          'email': { 'remote': 'That email address has already
                                been registered.' }
          }
        });
      });
    </script>
  </head>
  <body>
    <form id="registration_form"
          method="post"
          action="form.submit.php">
      <table>
        <tr><th>Email</th><td><input name="email" /></td></tr>
        <tr><th>Password</th><td><input id="password"
                                        type="password"
                                        name="password" /></td></tr>
        <tr><th>Password (repeat)</th>
          <td><input type="password" name="password2" /></td>
        </tr>
        <tr><th colspan="2"><input type="submit" /></th></tr>
      </table>
    </form>
  </body>
</html>
```

If you wish, you could set up the `messages` object on the server side the same way as the `rules` object is created.

Notice that the first password element has both a `name` and an `id`. The `id` is for the `equalTo` validation on `password2` because `equalTo` checks against an input with the specified `id`, and the `name` is there because all HTML form elements require names, or they will not submit their data.

The form is not yet complete, as the `remote` check requires us to write a handler for it on the server.

Server-side code

For the remote email test, we will need to create a file that compares the email value against existing data (for the purpose of the example, we will need to pretend that we're checking a real database of already-registered email addresses). I've created a very simple example here, which simply echoes `false` if you have entered `kae@verens.com` and `true` otherwise. Save it as `form.check-email.php`:

```php
<?php
  if(isset($_GET['email']) && $_GET['email']=='kae@verens.com')
    echo 'false';
  else echo 'true';
?>
```

For your own usage, you might want to compare the requested email address against your own database. Just remember to output `false` if the email address exists in your database, or `true` if it's not there.

Your client-side code is complete now—it should validate against the password fields and the `remote` email checker.

The final part is to validate the form using PHP when it is finally submitted.

You can use the same `form.submit.php` file as in the last example. We just need to add new rules for `remote` and `equalTo`.

The remote rule needs some thought, as it is inefficient to have your PHP script make an HTTP request to a file that is probably in the same directory as the requester. Instead, you could create a second PHP file for checking the email when called locally, named `form.check-email-local.php` (note the `-local`—we'll use that in a moment):

```php
<?php
  if($value=='kae@verens.com')return false;
  else return true;
?>
```

An interesting thing about the PHP include statement is that it can be treated like a function — you can return true or false from it, and that will immediately end execution of the script and return the true or false value to the line that included it.

Using this, combined with the simple addition of -local to the file's name, we get this addition to form.submit.php, in the get_errors function:

```
// verify that 'email' inputs are valid email addresses
if(isset($rule['email']) && $rule['email']
    && !filter_var($value,FILTER_VALIDATE_EMAIL))
  $errors[]=$hname.' must be an email address.';
// check that two input fields are equal
if(isset($rule['equalTo'])){
  $ename=substr($rule['equalTo'],1);
  if(!isset($form_data[$ename]) || $value!=$form_data[$ename])
    $errors[]=$hname.' must equal '.htmlspecialchars($ename);
}
// check a value against a remote file
if(isset($rule['remote'])){
  $fn=preg_replace('/\.php$/','-local.php',$rule['remote']);
  if(!(include $fn))$errors[]=$hname.'
    .htmlspecialchars($value).' is already registered';
}
$rules[$name]['found']=true;
```

Large select boxes

Many forms have a select box in them that is very large, source-wise. For example, a country select box that names all the countries in the world.

In Chapter 2, *Quick Tricks*, I described how to load up the second select box based on the value of a first select box. In this section, I'll describe how to load up the first select box through Ajax.

In many cases, it is possible to select a default value that is correct for most visitors. For example, if I was working on an Irish website and a contact form needed the visitor's country to be entered, it would be safe to assume that Ireland should be the default, and the visitor can change it if they need to.

This allows us to do something interesting. Instead of printing out the entire list of countries into a select box, it is only necessary to print one, and to load up the full list only if the select box is actually touched by the visitor (click or focus). This is great for long forms that have many large select boxes.

Client-side code

We will use the same form as in the last example, so copy `form.php` from the previous example.

Add a row to the form table with a select box in it, using:

```
<tr>
  <th>Country</th>
  <td>
    <select name="country">
      <option selected="selected">Ireland</option>
    </select>
  </td>
</tr>
```

This should give you a form looking similar to the following:

The important thing to note here is that there is only one option available in it. There's no need to provide more if you don't think it will need to change for most people. Another very important thing is that the default that you expect people to click is actually that one value. Even if you don't expect people to change it, you still need to provide the default so that when the form is submitted, the default is submitted as well. In order to have the box populate itself when it is activated, you need to add some behavior to it.

Change the `$(document).ready` function in the head section of the document to this:

```
$(document).ready(function(){
  $('#registration_form').validate({
    'rules': <?php echo json_encode($form_rules); ?>,
    'messages': {
      'email': { 'remote': 'That email address has already been
                  registered.' }
    }
  });
  $('select[name="country"]').focus(function(){
    if($('option',this).length<2)
      $.getJSON('form.countries.php?country=' +
      $(this).attr('value'),form_setCountries);
  });
});
```

```
function form_setCountries(res){
  $('select[name="country"]')
    .html(res.html)
    .attr('selectedIndex',res.index);
}
```

Notice the $('option',this) part. This construct tells jQuery to select all option elements that are contained within this (the select[name="country"] element), and if there are less than two items in the collection, then get the list of countries from the server.

The list is returned as a JSON object with two parameters:

- An HTML parameter, which is the list of options formatted as HTML
- An index parameter, which tells the select box where in the new list it will find the item that was selected before the list changed

The index parameter works around a bug where the browser will not pre-select an item in the new list even if there is a selected="selected" parameter in its HTML.

Server-side code

On the PHP end, it's simply a matter of outputting the list of countries in <option> elements.

Save this file as form.countries.php:

```php
<?php
$selected=$_GET['country'];
$countries=array(
   'Ireland', 'Scotland', 'Northern Ireland',
   'Wales', 'Britain'
);
$html='';
$i=$index=0;
foreach($countries as $country){
   if($country==$selected)$index=$i;
   $html.='<option>'.htmlspecialchars($country).'</option>';
   $i++;
}
echo "{'html':'".addslashes($html)."','index':$index}";
```

I've only included a short list of countries here for demonstration purposes. In reality, you would use this trick only for very large select boxes. Any less than, say, 10 items in the select box, and it's probably not worth it, as the overhead of the JavaScript that updates the select box virtually guarantees you're wasting bandwidth.

Now when the select box is clicked for the first time, it grabs the required options from the server:

Auto-suggestion

In some cases, you will want to provide a combo box. That's a select box where there is a number of predefined options, but the user can enter a new option by hand if it is not in the list.

An example use of this is a search form. Some search boxes are written in such a way that you can start writing something, and a box will appear below the search box with a list of possible existing searches that you might have meant. The following image shows what happens when I write **jqu** into the search box in Firefox and then pause for a moment:

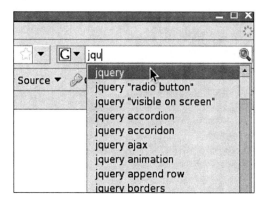

In Chapter 2, *Quick Tricks*, dynamically filling a second select box was shown, but that depends on the server having all of the values in its database. In the case of countries and cities, and especially in the case of cities and towns, it is unfeasible to do this realistically, because of the sheer number of them, and also because the list sometimes changes—new towns are constantly being created, so any static form will quickly become inaccurate.

For simplicity's sake, we will handle just cities in this example. A more complete example could also include towns, but that would basically result in the same code being repeated. You can complete it for towns as an exercise, saving the values to a database.

Client-side code

Copy all of the files from the previous example into a new directory. Then edit the form.php file to add a new row to the table:

```
<tr><th>City</th><td><input name="city" /></td></tr>
```

And in the $(document).ready function, add the following code:

```
$('input[name="city"]').keyup(form_citySearch);
```

This line tells jQuery to run the form_citySearch function every time a key is pressed in the input box.

And in the main <script> element, add the following functions:

```
function form_citySearch(){
  var country=$('select[name="country"]').attr('value');
  var txt=$('input[name="city"]').attr('value');
  $.getJSON('form.cities.php?country=' +
    country + '&city=' + txt,
    form_citySearch_show
  );
}
function form_citySearch_show(res){
  if($('#citysearch_list'))$('#citysearch_list').remove();
  if(!res.cities || !res.cities.length)return;
  var el=$('input[name="city"]');
  var pos=$('input[name="city"]').position();
  var style='position:absolute;left:' + pos.left +
    'px;top:' + (pos.top+el.height()) +
    'px;border:1px solid #000;background:#fff';
  var html='';
  for(idx in res.cities){
    var city=res.cities[idx];
    html+='<a onclick="$(\'input[name=city]\')' +
```

```
            '.attr(\'value\',\'' + city + '\')">' + city +
            '</a><br />';
        }
        $('<div id="citysearch_list" style="' + style + '">' +
          html + '</div>').appendTo(el[0].parentNode);
        $(document.body).click(function(){
          $('#citysearch_list').remove();
        });
    }
```

Whenever you press a key in the city input box, the `form_citySearch` function is called. This function checks the selected country and the text that's already written into the city field, and sends them both to the server, to get a list of possible results.

When results are received, it's expected that an array of cities is returned—`res.cities`. HTML for a number of links is created from that list and shown on-screen below the input box. When clicked, the link that's clicked will insert the selected item into the field.

In order to complete it, then, we need to provide the server-side code.

Server-side code

Create a file named `form.cities.php`, containing this:

```
<?php
$cities=array(
  'Ireland'=>array(
    'Carlow', 'Cavan', 'Clare', 'Cork', 'Donegal', 'Dublin',
    'Galway', 'Kerry', 'Kildare', 'Kilkenny', 'Laois', 'Leitrim',
    'Limerick', 'Longford', 'Louth', 'Mayo', 'Meath', 'Monaghan',
    'Offaly', 'Roscommon', 'Sligo', 'Tipperary', 'Waterford',
    'Westmeath', 'Wexford', 'Wicklow'
  )
);
$found=array();
if(isset($cities[$_GET['country']])){
  $txt=strtolower($_GET['city']);
  $len=strlen($txt);
  foreach($cities[$_GET['country']] as $city){
    if(substr(strtolower($city),0,$len)===$txt)
      $found[]=addslashes($city);
  }
}
echo "{'cities':[";
if(count($found))echo "'".join("','",$found)."'";
echo "]}";
```

Cities are provided for Ireland in this case (actually, they're counties, but that doesn't matter for the purpose of the example). In a real-life example, you might obtain the list from a database.

Try this one out by typing 'C' into the cities box when Ireland is selected:

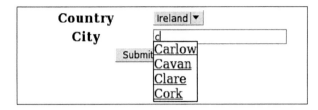

Then try adding an '**a**'. You will see that the number of available choices narrows down.

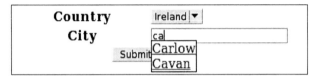

Clicking one of the choices will set the field value equal to it.

We're not done yet. One annoyance with the way I've shown this is that every time you press a key, an HTTP request is shot off. This will cause problems; especially if you're a fast typist and the server is far away. You will have the auto-suggest box appearing and changing as you type.

Client-side code

The solution is to do the search only after there's a pause of, say, 500 ms. Half a second is a legitimate pause for an average typer.

In the $(document).ready function, change the keyup behavior to this:

```
$('input[name="city"]').keyup(form_citySearch_delayed);
```

And then add this function to the main `<script>` element.

```
function form_citySearch_delayed(){
  if(window.citySearchTimeout)
    clearTimeout(window.citySearchTimeout);
  window.citySearchTimeout=setTimeout(form_citySearch,500);
}
```

What it does, is to set a 500 ms delay before doing the request. However, if another `keyup` event happens, it will clear the previous timeout and start a new one. It is very important to clear the previous timeout—otherwise you're not solving the problem, just delaying it.

Summary

In this chapter, we explored how to validate forms using jQuery and PHP, how to set up the validation rules form a single configuration kept in PHP, and remote validation.

Then we also looked into enhancing some existing form controls, optimizing a large select box, and creating an auto-suggest field.

In the next chapter, we will discuss how you can manage creating, uploading, editing, moving, downloading, and deleting files and directories.

5
File Management

File management can be a very large project, depending on how advanced you want to go. In this chapter, we will look at the most common file management functions using PHP and jQuery, such as:

- Creating, editing, and deleting directories
- Uploading, downloading, and deleting files
- Moving files and directories to other directories

These file management functions will be accomplished using a select box that can be used in any form requiring file selection.

Security

We have not discussed security much in the previous chapters. This is because it is assumed that you are a good programmer and know what you're doing. There are some points about file management that need to be re-iterated, though—anything that affects files on the server is a weak point and will be targeted by crackers.

If possible, never allow the user to decide the name of the file on the server. For example, if the uploaded file is meant to be a profile photo, rename the file based on the user's ID (or some other criteria).

To demonstrate why this is important, try this example—create a text file with the following contents, name it `test.php.jpg`, and view it in your browser:

```php
<?php
  echo 'hello world';
?>
```

When viewed in the browser, you will see that the server executes the file as PHP, instead of attempting to display it as an image, or even sending it as plain text to the browser:

> **http://play/php_...le/test.php.jpg**
>
> hello world

What is alarming about this scenario is that most developers check only the last extension of the filename, but in Apache, if **MultiViews** is enabled, then all extensions are examined, and in this case, a default installation of Apache will assume that the .jpg extension in the filename is actually a language indicator and that the real extension is .php.

There are two solutions in this case—turn off **MultiViews** in your Apache configuration or check all extensions of every file that is uploaded. I prefer the latter, as you cannot be certain that your script will always be on a server with **MultiViews** turned off.

If you are accepting file uploads, then at a minimum, you should consider either restricting the filenames to a set of extensions that you trust or banning a set of extensions that you mistrust. As shown in the test.php.jpg example, you must not test just the last extension. Either ban multiple extensions altogether, or test all of them.

When accepting a file for upload, there are two things that need to be checked—what is the filename and where it is to be placed. You need to be very careful not to allow people to upload files that can be executed on the server (for example, .php files), and not to allow files to be uploaded to places where they shouldn't go (for example, test/../../../../etc/passwd).

Ideally, uploaded files should be kept in a directory that is not accessible using a straightforward URL. For example, if your web root is /home/kae/public_html on the server, then keep your files in /home/kae/uploaded_files. That way, even if the uploaded files are .php scripts or other executables, they cannot be executed because they are not within the web-accessible directory. Serve the files using a script (described later in this chapter).

Choosing a directory

There are a number of ways of allowing a directory to be selected. We could build a tree menu or an icon-based navigation system, like Windows, KDE, Gnome, which is popular in common desktop managers. For the purpose of this chapter, a tree-based solution is too bulky. We will look at how to build a tree-based navigation tree in Chapter 7, *Image Manipulation*.

In this chapter, we will build a select box that can be used in a form for file selection and uploads. The select box will change dynamically as different options are selected.

To set this up, start by creating a new directory, which is outside of the web root, and make sure it is writeable by the server. For this chapter's example, let's set the directory permissions to be fully open. When putting this directory on a live server, make sure it is tied down to allow just the web server to change its contents.

On my test server, the directory I am testing with is `/home/kae/uploaded_files`, and within this directory I have two more directories, `dir1` and `dir2`. For testing purposes, I've also placed two directories `dir3` and `dir4` inside `dir1`. You should replicate this on your own test server as well.

Client-side code

The goal of this chapter is to produce a very simple select box that, when combined with jQuery and PHP, will act as a mini file manager as well as a file/directory selector.

So, to start off, let's create a simple select box. Place the following HTML in a file in a new example directory and call it `file_manager.html`:

```html
<html>
  <head>
    <script src="../jquery.min.js"></script>
    <script src="file_manager.js"></script>
  </head>
  <body>
    <form action="#">
      <select name="selected_file">
        <option>/dir1/</option>
      </select>
    </form>
  </body>
</html>
```

Note that there is one single value in the select box. This is similar to the idea discussed in the previous chapter, where we should print only what we absolutely need to. We don't need to see the entire file structure of the server, so we just print the directory we are interested in.

We want to populate the select box with its parent directories, and also to list the directories below it. To do this, add the following script and save it as `file_manager.js` (already referenced in the preceding HTML):

```javascript
function fm_getFiles(){
  var fname=$('select[name="selected_file"]').attr('value');
  $.getJSON('file_manager.php?f='+fname,fm_updateValues);
}
function fm_updateValues(vals){
  $('select[name="selected_file"]')
    .html(vals.options)
    .attr('selectedIndex',vals.selectedIndex);
}
$(document).ready(function(){
  fm_getFiles();
  $('select[name="selected_file"]').change(fm_getFiles);
});
```

Don't test this yet, as it will require some PHP to complete it.

What will happen here is that when the document is ready, the jQuery runs the fm_getFiles function, which checks the current value of the select box and requests the directory listing from the server. This listing is sent back to the fm_updateValues function, which adds the directories to the select box and resets the selected select box.

Visually, what will happen is that the select box will get a little bit wider to accommodate the width of the subdirectory names.

Server-side code

On the server, all we need to do is accept the requested directory and print its parent directories and subdirectories (and itself).

Save this in file_manager.php:

```php
<?php
  $base='/home/kae/uploaded_files/';
// if using a Windows server, an example $base is:
// $base='c:/wamp/kae/uploaded_files/';

// make sure that a file or directory is requested
  if(!isset($_REQUEST['f'])) exit;
// { sanitize input
  $f=preg_replace('#^/*|/(/)|/$#','\1',$_REQUEST['f']);
  if(preg_match('#(^|/)\.\./#',$f))exit;
// }
// { check that selected directory actually exists
  if(!file_exists($base.$f)) exit;
  if(!is_dir($base.$f)) exit;
// }

  $parent_dirs=array();
  $child_dirs=array();
  $selectedIndex=0;
  $options='<optgroup label="Directories">';
// { generate parents array
  if($f!=''){
    $ps=explode('/',preg_replace('#/[^/]*$#','','/'.$f));
    foreach($ps as $p) $parent_dirs[]=$p;
    if(count($ps)){
      $tmp='/';
      foreach($ps as $p){
        $tmp.=$p==''?'':$p.'/';
        $selectedIndex++;
        $options.='<option>' .htmlspecialchars($tmp) .'</option>';
      }
```

```
      }
    }
// }
// { selected directory
  $options.='<option selected="selected">'
    .htmlspecialchars($f?'/'.$f:'')
    .'/</option>';
// }
// { generate child directories
  $d=new DirectoryIterator($base.$f);
  foreach($d as $sd){
    if($sd->isDot())continue;
    if(is_dir($base.$f.'/'.$sd))$child_dirs[]=$sd->getFilename();
  }
  if(count($child_dirs)){
    $tf=$f?$f.'/':'';
    natsort($child_dirs);
    foreach($child_dirs as $cd){
      $options.='<option>/'
        .htmlspecialchars($tf.$cd).'/</option>';
    }
  }
// }
  $options.='</optgroup>';

  echo json_encode(array(
    'options'=>$options,
    'selectedIndex'=>$selectedIndex,
  ));
?>
```

The first highlighted line is your documents area — the area on the server to store your files. It needs to be writeable by the server and the value must end with /. Later in the chapter we will discuss files, so make sure that the directory is located *outside* the web root — web browsers should not be able to access the files directly.

The next highlighted section is to make sure that the client doesn't try sending through values that it shouldn't be sending.

After that, the replacement `<option>` elements are created for the select box, in the following three sections:

- The parent directories
- The selected directory
- The child directories of the selected directory

The code lists the full names of the directories, relative to the base directory configured in the first line.

 In this chapter, I'm not reporting any errors back to the client—it would make the examples more complex. You could do that as an exercise for yourself. If you face any problems, be sure to check your web server's error logs.

When clicked, the select box will look like this:

And here is what it looks like when / is clicked:

You can see that the manager doesn't show anything more than the current directory's parents and children. When / is selected, the children of **/dir1/** are no longer visible. When **/dir1/** was selected, any siblings in its parent directories were not visible. The reason for this is that, if we were to show the entire navigation tree in the select box, then it would be too large to be easily usable, and that's *before* we add filenames to the select box.

Creating, renaming, and deleting directories

Let's say we want to create/rename/delete directories apart from the root directory, /, which should of course never be renamed or deleted.

Keeping with the compact theme, this example involves adding a select box with a list of actions that can be performed on the selected directory.

In the HTML, all that should be changed is the `<option>` element—we defined /dir1/ as being selected in the last example, but as we are adding the ability to delete directories, it's best to set the value in this example to a directory that cannot be deleted. In your own production code, you should make sure the selected directory exists before printing it out to the select box. In this example, it's plain HTML, so there will be no checking beforehand.

```
<select name="selected_file"><option>/</option></select>
```

The real action happens in the PHP and JavaScript.

Client-side code

All of the following JavaScript changes should be applied to the `file_manager.js` file:

1. Change the `$(document).ready` function to insert an action select box after the directory selector as follows:

    ```
    $(document).ready(function(){
      fm_getFiles();
      $('select[name="selected_file"]').change(fm_getFiles);
      $('<select id="selected_file_options"></select>')
        .insertAfter($('select[name="selected_file"]'))
        .change(fm_runAction);
    });
    ```

    What it does is to add a select box that, when changed, runs the `fm_runAction` function.

    The select box is not populated at the moment. It should be populated based on the directory selected.

2. Add this to the end of the `fm_updateValues` function:

    ```
    fm_changeOptions();
    ```

And here is the `fm_changeOptions` function:

```
function fm_changeOptions(){
  var html='<option> -- </option>';
  var val=$('select[name="selected_file"]').attr('value');
  html+='<option>new sub-directory</option>';
  if(val!='/'){
    html+='<option>rename directory</option>'
        +'<option>delete directory</option>';
  }
  $('#selected_file_options').html(html);
}
```

This renders a select box similar to the following when a directory is selected:

3. When this select box is changed, the `fm_runAction` function is run:

```
function fm_runAction(){
  switch($('#selected_file_options').attr('value')){
    case 'new sub-directory':
      fm_addSubdirectory();
      break;
    case 'rename directory':
      fm_renameDirectory();
      break;
    case 'delete directory':
      fm_deleteDirectory();
      break;
  }
}
```

All this does is to run another function based on the selected option.

   ° If **new sub-directory** is selected, this function is run:

```
function fm_addSubdirectory(){
  var n=prompt('new sub-directory\'s name:');
  if(!n) return;
```

```
    if(/[^a-zA-Z-_0-9 ]/.test(n)) return alert('invalid
character(s). please only use a-z, A-Z, -, _, 0-9, or
space');
    var fname=$('select[name="selected_file"]').attr('value');
    $.getJSON(
        'file_manager.php?f='+fname+'&a=newDir&n='+n,
        fm_updateValues);
}
```

And it opens this pop up:

- ○ If **rename directory** is selected, this function is run:

```
function fm_renameDirectory(){
    var fname=$('select[name="selected_file"]').attr('value');
    var n=prompt(
        'rename directory to what?',
        fname.replace(/.*\/(.*)\/$/,'$1'));
    if(!n)return;
    if(/[^a-zA-Z-_0-9 ]/.test(n))
        return alert('invalid character(s).
            please only use a-z, A-Z, -, _, 0-9, or space');
    $.getJSON(
        'file_manager.php?f='+fname+'&a=renameDir&n=
            '+n,
        fm_updateValues);
}
```

Now, the **rename directory** option looks like this:

- ○ If **delete directory** is selected, this function is run:

```
function fm_deleteDirectory(){
  if(!confirm(
    'are you sure you want to delete this directory?'
  ))return;
  var fname=$('select[name="selected_file"]').attr('value');
  $.getJSON(
    'file_manager.php?f='+fname+'&a=delDir',
    fm_updateValues);
}
```

This function verifies that you do want to delete the directory. It is very important to always verify before deletion. That way you can be sure that someone who deletes a directory by accident has a second chance to change his or her mind before doing it.

The first two functions request a directory name, only allowing alphanumeric and other simple characters as the inputs.

After the checks, each of the functions requests the server to complete the acts and return the result to the `fm_updateValues` function, which will update the directory selector box.

Server-side code

On the server side, all we need to change is add the action code before the list of directories is re-built. So, add this after the initial checks in the `file_manager.php` file, and before the `$parent_dirs=array();` statement:

```php
if(isset($_REQUEST['a'])){
  switch($_REQUEST['a']){
    case 'newDir': // {
      if(!isset($_REQUEST['n'])) exit;
      $n=$_REQUEST['n'];
      if(preg_match('#[^a-zA-Z0-9-_ ]#',$n) || !strlen($n)) exit;
      mkdir($base.$f.'/'.$n);
      if(file_exists($base.$f.'/'.$n) && is_dir($base.$f.'/'.$n))
        $f=$f?$f.'/'.$n:$n;
      break;
    // }
    case 'renameDir': // {
      if(!isset($_REQUEST['n'])) exit;
      $n=$_REQUEST['n'];
      if(preg_match('#[^a-zA-Z0-9-_ ]#',$n) || !strlen($n)) exit;
      if(!$f || $f=='/') exit;
      $fp=strpos($f,'/')!==false
        ?preg_replace('#(.*/)[^/]*$#','$1',$f)
        :'';
      if(file_exists($base.$fp.$n)) exit;
      rename($base.$f,$base.$fp.$n);
      mkdir($base.$f.'/'.$n);
      if(file_exists($base.$fp.$n) && is_dir($base.$fp.$n))
        $f=$fp.$n;
      break;
    // }
    case 'delDir': // {
      if(!$f || $f=='/') exit;
      $fp=strpos($f,'/')!==false
                      ?preg_replace('#(.*/)[^/]*$#','$1',$f):'';
      rmdir($base.$f);
      if(!file_exists($base.$f)) $f=$fp;
      break;
    // }
  }
  $f=str_replace('//','/',$f);
}
```

Each action has its own section in the `switch` block. The action is performed and `$f` (the selected directory) is reset if need be. For example, if a directory is created, `$f` is set to the new directory; if deleted, `$f` is set to the parent; and if renamed, then `$f` is set to the new name.

You should take some time to read through the code here. Every action that changes a file on the server has the potential to be a target for a hacker, so it's important that you are familiar with the code that does the changes, and you are happy that each line does its job as well as it can.

> I'll reiterate that the base directory being manipulated here *must* be kept out of the website's document root. And again, no errors are returned to the client, to simplify the example. In the previous example, it was unlikely that you would encounter any errors, but in this case, there are more potential errors that can happen. If using this in production code, please be sure to either return errors to the client, or log them using your PHP.

Moving directories

For moving, you need to provide a destination directory. To do this, this example will add a second directory-selector box when the **move** action is selected.

Client-side code

We will describe the JavaScript side of this function before writing the PHP.

First, replace the `$(document).ready` function in the `file_manager.js` file with this:

```
$(document).ready(function(){
  fm_getFiles();
  $('select[name="selected_file"]').change(function(){
    fm_getFiles();
  });
  $('<select id="selected_file_options"></select>')
    .insertAfter($('select[name="selected_file"]'))
    .change(fm_runAction);
  $('<span id="selected_file_extras"></span>')
    .insertAfter($('#selected_file_options'));
});
```

Note that we've changed the way the fm_getFiles function is called. In this example, we need to tell the fm_getFiles function which select box it needs to act on. To accomplish this, we will change the code so that if a parameter is supplied, it should use that parameter as a selector pointing to the box it should change and, if no parameter is supplied, then the function uses the directory selection box. To ensure that no parameter is sent, we change the code so that it very explicitly has no parameter set. (When an event fires, it calls its target function with some parameters, and we want to avoid that.)

The last line adds a new <span> after the action select box, which will be used to hold the new options for detailing moves.

To accommodate this new method of calling fm_getFiles, change it to this:

```
function fm_getFiles(selector){
  if(typeof selector!=='string')
    selector='select[name="selected_file"]';
  var fname=$(selector).attr('value');
  $.getJSON('file_manager.php?f='+fname,function(vals){
    vals.selector=selector;
    fm_updateValues(vals);
  });
}
```

Apart from setting the selector, note that the call to the server is changed slightly as well, by creating an inline function that adds the selector to vals before carrying on with the update.

> This is an example of a closure in which, the selector variable is referenced in the inline function even though the function will be called asynchronously some time after the containing function has been completed. In PHP, the selector variable would be unassigned immediately when the surrounding function was completed and left. However, with JavaScript, the variable is stored to be used by the inline function whenever it is eventually triggered. This is very useful for many situations. Closures will soon be available in PHP.

In fm_changeOptions, add the new move option by changing the appropriate lines to this:

```
if(val!='/'){
  html+='<option>rename directory</option>'
      +'<option>delete directory</option>'
      +'<option>move directory to</option>';
}
```

And in the `fm_runAction` function, add this case to the `switch` block:

```
case 'move directory to':
  fm_moveDirectorySetup();
  break;
```

So far, each action we've done required only a single function to get the relevant input and send it to the server.

In this case, though, the input is another directory, and so we will need to create a new select box for it:

```
function fm_moveDirectorySetup(){
  var orig=$('select[name="selected_file"]');
  var extras=$('#selected_file_extras');
  $('<select id="selected_file_todir" class="noactions"><option>'
     +orig.attr('value').replace(/[^\/]*\/$/,'')
     +'</option></select>')
    .appendTo(extras)
    .change(function(){
      fm_getFiles('#selected_file_todir');
    });
  $('<input type="button" value="move" />')
    .appendTo(extras)
    .click(fm_moveDirectory);
  fm_getFiles('#selected_file_todir');
}
```

This code creates a new select box and a submit button, and calls the `fm_getFiles` function with the new select box's selector.

Note that there is a `noactions` class in the new select box. The `fm_updateValues` function needs to be changed so that it doesn't try to add an action box to it.

```
function fm_updateValues(vals){
  var selector=(typeof vals.selector=='string')
    ?vals.selector
    :'select[name="selected_file"]';
  $(selector)
    .html(vals.options)
    .attr('selectedIndex',vals.selectedIndex);
  if(!$(selector).hasClass('noactions'))fm_changeOptions();
}
```

Now, it will call `fm_changeOptions` only if the select box it is working on doesn't have the `noactions` class. The reason we need to do this is that we're re-using the directory-choosing logic from the first select box, but we want to avoid adding a drop-down action after it, as it would make no sense. The `noactions` class is to tell the script that when changing the second directory, the select box should not change the drop-down action.

Just in case the action option is changed, we need to "clean up" the new select box and button, so add this to the end of the `fm_changeOptions` function:

```
$('#selected_file_extras').empty();
```

Now, when **move** is clicked, we can finally run the action, in the same way as the other actions were performed:

```
function fm_moveDirectory(){
  var from=$('select[name="selected_file"]').attr('value');
  var to=$('#selected_file_todir').attr('value');
  if(from==to || to.indexOf(from)==0)
    return alert('cannot move directory into itself');
  if(from.replace(/[^\/]*\/$/,'')==to)
    return alert('already in that directory');
  $.getJSON(
    'file_manager.php?f='+from+'&a=moveDir&t='+to,
    fm_updateValues);
}
```

We provide a few checks to save time (such as making sure directories are not moved into themselves), and then submit the change if nothing is wrong.

Server-side code

Surprisingly, after seeing the complexity of the JavaScript, the PHP for moving a directory just involves adding a new case to the `switch` block in the `file_manager.php` file:

```
case 'moveDir': // {
  if(!isset($_REQUEST['t'])) exit;
  $t=$_REQUEST['t'];
  $t=preg_replace('#^/*|/(/)|/$#','\1',$t);
```

```
    if(preg_match('#(^|/)\.\./#',$f)) exit;
    $n=$t.'/'.preg_replace('#.*/#','',$f);
    if(rename($base.$f,$base.$n)) $f=$t;
      break;
  // }
```

The $_REQUEST parameter t is used as the directory to be moved to.

We do some sanitization on the variable, the same way it's done on $f earlier in the file. And then the PHP function, rename, is asked to move the directory. If it fails, then it's for any number of reasons—you tried to move a directory into itself, permissions were denied, or the directory was already in the directory you wanted to move it to, and so on. In most cases, we can catch this on the client side before it gets that far, so don't worry about it. Log it if you think there's a problem.

If the move was successful, $f is set to the new address.

File uploads

There are a number of ways to upload files. The method used in this example depends on a bit of Flash. This is OK because these days, everyone except the staunchest diehards have Flash on their machines for watching videos online or whatever other purposes arise (and these staunch diehards probably frown at JavaScript anyway).

For this example, you will need to download a copy of the Uploadify plugin from http://www.uploadify.com/ and extract it into the root of your test server. In my case, I downloaded version 1.6.2. Uploadify has been around for a long time, and is well-regarded.

Ajax-based file uploads used to be tricky. The easiest method was to create a small form and submit it into a hidden iframe, which would then report back to the main application when the file is uploaded. These days, the most popular method is to use a JavaScript bridge into Flash, which does not need the iframe or the form, and can also manage multiple uploads natively.

Client-side code

We will need to make a change to the HTML. We need to add the Uploadify plugin, and also add a minor piece of CSS to make it look OK. Add this to the file_manager.html file:

```
<script src="../jquery.uploadify-v1.6.2/jquery.uploadify.js">
</script>
```

```
<style type="text/css">
  embed{
    position:relative;
    top:7px;
  }
</style>
```

For some reason, on my Firefox test browser, the **Browse** button is shifted up a few pixels—the CSS fixes that.

As part of the upload example, we'll also need to add the ability to list existing files. Change `fm_getFiles` in the `file_manager.js` file so that it doesn't do anything if the requested directory is actually a file (all directories in the file manager have a / at the end of them):

```
function fm_getFiles(selector){
  if(typeof selector!=='string')
    selector='select[name="selected_file"]';
  var fname=$(selector).attr('value');
  if(fname=='' || /\/$/.test(fname)){
    $.getJSON('file_manager.php?f='+fname,function(vals){
      vals.selector=selector;
      fm_updateValues(vals);
    });
  }
  else fm_changeOptions();
}
```

In the case of files, we skip the `fm_updateValues` function and go straight to the `fm_changeOptions` function to list the options available to files (as shown highlighted).

The changes we need to make in the `fm_changeOptions` function are:

```
function fm_changeOptions(){
  var html='<option> -- </option>';
  var val=$('select[name="selected_file"]').attr('value');
  var is_dir=/\/$/.test(val);
  if(is_dir){
    html+='<option>new sub-directory</option>'
        +'<option>upload file</option>';
    if(val!='/'){
      html+='<option>rename directory</option>'
          +'<option>delete directory</option>'
          +'<option>move directory to</option>';
    }
  }
}
```

```
    $('#selected_file_options').html(html);
    $('#selected_file_extras').empty();
}
```

We start with the -- option common to everything, then check if the selected node is a file or a directory, and show the options appropriate to the choice.

For this, we just need to add one more case in the fm_runAction function:

```
case 'upload file':
    fm_uploadFileSetup();
    break;
```

And here is the fm_uploadFileSetup function:

```
function fm_uploadFileSetup(){
    var extras=$('#selected_file_extras');
    $('<input id="fm_file" type="hidden" />')
        .appendTo(extras)
    $('#fm_file').fileUpload ({
        'uploader':'../jquery.uploadify-v1.6.2/uploader.swf',
        'script':'file_manager.php',
        'cancelImg':'../jquery.uploadify-v1.6.2/cancel.png',
        'auto':true,
        'multi':true,
        'buttonImg':'browse.png',
        'scriptData': {
            'f':$('select[name="selected_file"]').attr('value'),
            'a':'uploadFile'
        },
        'fileDataName':'file',
        'width':79,
        'height':23,
        'onComplete':function(a,b,c,d,e){
            fm_updateValues(eval('('+d+')'));
        }
    });
}
```

Note the highlighted lines. The first two should point to the correct files in the version of Uploadify you downloaded. The last one is a replacement browse image. Because uploader is a Flash application, it does not use HTML elements, so we need to create an upload button to be used. In my case, I created an image of a button by getting a screenshot of an HTML file, which contained just this:

```
<input type="button" value="browse..." />
```

When this file is rendered in a browser and a screenshot of this is saved as
browse.png in your test directory, choose the **download** option in the action box.
The example application will look like this:

When the **browse...** button is clicked, you can select files to upload. In fact, you can
select multiple files.

Before uploading these selected files, we need to write the server-side code.

Server-side code

First, add this case to the switch block in the file_manager.php file to handle
the upload:

```
case 'uploadFile': // {
  if(!isset($_FILES['file'])) exit;
  $n=$_FILES['file']['name'];
  if(preg_match('#/|\.\.#',$n)) exit;
  move_uploaded_file(
    $_FILES['file']['tmp_name'],
    $base.$f.'/'.$n
  );
  break;
// }
```

Add this to the small block of array initializations after that:

```
$child_files=array();
```

And in the "generate child directories" block, add this line before the end of the first `foreach` loop:

```
else $child_files[]=$sd->getFilename();
```

After the end of the `<optgroup>` definition, just before the `json_encode` line, we will add the files to the options list:

```
$options.='<optgroup label="Files">';
if(count($child_files)){
  $tf=$f?$f.'/':'';
  natsort($child_files);
  foreach($child_files as $cd){
    $options.='<option>/'
      .htmlspecialchars($tf.$cd)
      .'</option>';
  }
}
$options.='</optgroup>';
```

That's it. Now, when file is uploaded, it will be added to the options list.

Here is what the directory or files selector looks like after uploading some files into the `/dir1/` directory:

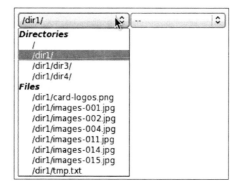

I think you'll agree that this list looks a lot better than when it contained just directories!

Renaming, deleting, and moving files

This can be done using almost exactly the same code that the directories used. In fact, that's how I did it. Instead of writing everything twice, I added some code to differentiate between directories and files when necessary.

Client-side code

In the `fm_changeOptions` function in the `file_manager.js` file, add an `else` clause to the `if(is_dir)` block:

```
else{
  html+='<option>rename file</option>'
       +'<option>delete file</option>'
       +'<option>move file to</option>';
}
```

Change the `fm_runAction` function so that there are cases for each of these options:

```
function fm_runAction(){
  $('#selected_file_extras').empty();
  switch($('#selected_file_options').attr('value')){
    case 'new sub-directory':
      fm_addSubdirectory();
      break;
    case 'rename directory':
    case 'rename file':
      fm_renameDirectory();
      break;
    case 'delete directory':
    case 'delete file':
      fm_deleteDirectory();
      break;
    case 'move directory to':
    case 'move file to':
      fm_moveDirectorySetup();
      break;
    case 'upload file':
      fm_uploadFileSetup();
      break;
  }
}
```

Note that each new file action is actually run using the equivalent directory function. There are only minor changes left to make to those functions.

In the `fm_renameDirectory` function, change the prompt to be less about directories:

```
var n=prompt(
  'rename to what?',
  fname.replace(/.*\/(.*)\/?$/,'$1')
);
```

Note the ? at the end of the regular expression—it's needed because files don't have /
at the end.

Also, change the filename test in this function so that it allows dots:

```
if(/[^a-zA-Z-_0-9 .]/.test(n))
    return alert('invalid character(s). please only use a-z, A-Z,'
    +' -, _, ., 0-9, or space'
    );
```

Again, change the confirmation message in the fm_deleteDirectory function to:

```
if(!confirm('are you sure you want to delete this?'))return;
```

And finally, in the fm_moveDirectory function, add a ? to the end of filename test as
follows:

```
+orig.attr('value').replace(/[^\/]*\/?$/,'')
```

Server-side code

On the server side, most of the code is fine. There are just a few lines that need to be
changed to cater for files.

First, remove the following line from the beginning of the file_manager.php file—it
is no longer needed:

```
if(!is_dir($base.$f))exit;
```

In the renameDir block, change the regular expression to allow dots:

```
if(preg_match('#[^a-zA-Z0-9-_ .]#',$n)
```

And at the end of the same block, change the if statement to this:

```
if(file_exists($base.$fp.$n)){
    if(is_dir($base.$fp.$n))$f=$fp.$n;
    else $f=$fp;
}
```

This changes the $f variable to the directory containing the file, instead of the file
itself. Otherwise, the resulting list of directories and files would be empty (files don't
contain other files or directories).

In the delDir section, replace the rmdir($base.$f); statement with this:

```
if(is_dir($base.$f))rmdir($base.$f);
else unlink($base.$f);
```

And finally, at the end of the `switch` block, after the `str_replace` statement, add this:

```
$f=preg_replace('#^/|/$#','',$f);
```

That strips out any leading or following slashes that might have been introduced by the switch manipulations.

That's mostly it: a fully functional file manager that allows files to be uploaded, directories to be created, and everything to be manipulated, moved, or destroyed.

The only thing that's missing is allowing files to be downloaded.

File downloads

Instead of having to write a series of PHP pages that allow you to choose and then download a file, wouldn't it be great if you could just navigate to the file using the tiny application we've developed and have the file download itself?

The method we will use here is that, when a file is selected to be downloaded, the browser will be told by the JavaScript to add a new iframe to the HTML document, which will be linked to the file through the `file_manager.php` script. When the browser requests the file, the script will return the file, but with a `Content-type` header value, `application/octet-stream`, which the browser will not know how to use. This will cause the browser to ask the reader if the file should be downloaded.

So, here's how it's done.

Client-side code

In the `fm_changeOptions` function, change the `move file to` line to this:

```
            +'<option>move file to</option>'
            +'<option>download</option>';
```

Add this case to the `fm_runAction` function:

```
        case 'download':
          fm_download();
          break;
```

And now, here's where the magic happens:

```
function fm_download(){
  var fname=$('select[name="selected_file"]').attr('value');
  var extras=$('#selected_file_extras');
  $('<iframe src="file_manager.php?f='+fname+'&a=download">
```

```
      </iframe>')
    .css({'display':'none'})
    .appendTo(extras);
}
```

What this does is to create a hidden iframe, which requests the file from the server.

Server-side code

On the server, all you need to do is to add this new case to the action block:

```
case 'download': // {
  if(is_dir($base.$f))exit;
  $n=preg_replace('#.*/#','',$f);
  header('Content-Description: File Transfer');
  header('Content-Type: application/octet-stream');
  header('Content-Disposition: attachment; filename='
    .basename($base.$f));
  header('Content-Transfer-Encoding: binary');
  header('Expires: 0');
  header('Content-Control: must-revalidate, '
    .'post-check=0, pre-check=0');
  header('Pragma: public');
  header('Content-Length: ' . filesize($base.$f));
  ob_clean();
  flush();
  readfile($file);
  exit;
// }
```

This is fairly standard code and is taken almost verbatim from the `php.net` site.

Now when you choose a file to download, the following message pops up and asks you to save the file instead of displaying in the browser, which might happen ordinarily if it was an image or a text file, or any other similar file:

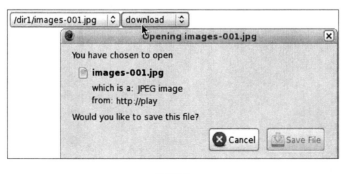

A complete file manager in about 8 kilobytes un-minimized! You might like to take the examples here and see how small it can get through abstraction of functions. There are certainly enough repeated sections to make a bit of a difference.

Summary

In this chapter, we walked through the creation of a file manager, which allows us to create, rename, move, and delete files and directories.

In the next chapter, we will build a weekly calendar, with events that can be created, edited, moved around, and deleted. We will also include recurring events in it.

6
Calendars

There are many reasons why you would want to display a calendar. You can use it to display upcoming events, to keep a diary, or to show a timetable. Recently, for example, I combined a calendar with an online store for a client to book meetings and receive payments more intuitively.

Google calendar is probably what springs to mind when people think of calendars online. There is a very good plugin called `jquery-week-calendar` that shows a week with events in a fashion similar to Google's calendar.

Its homepage is at `http://www.redredred.com.au/projects/ jquery-week-calendar/`.

In this chapter, we will use the `jquery-week-calendar` plugin to create and edit normal and recurring events.

To get the latest copy of the plugin, go to `http://code.google.com/p/ jquery-week-calendar/downloads/list` and get the highest-numbered file. The examples in this chapter are done with version 1.2.0.

Download the library and extract it so that there is a directory named
`jquery-weekcalendar-1.2.0` in the root of your demo directory.

In this chapter, we will discuss the following topics:

- Displaying a calendar for a week
- Creating and saving an event in that calendar
- Moving, editing, and deleting events
- Creating recurring events
- Editing and removing recurring events

Displaying the calendar

As usual, the HTML for the simplest configuration is very simple. Save this
as `calendar.html`:

```
<html>
 <head>
  <script src="../jquery.min.js"></script>
  <script src="../jquery-ui.min.js"></script>
  <script src="../jquery-weekcalendar-1.2.0/jquery.weekcalendar.js">
  </script>
  <script src="calendar.js"></script>
  <link rel="stylesheet" type="text/css"
        href="../jquery-ui.css" />
  <link rel="stylesheet" type="text/css"
        href="../jquery-weekcalendar-1.2.0/jquery.weekcalendar.css"/>
 </head>
 <body>
  <div id="calendar_wrapper" style="height:500px"></div>
 </body>
</html>
```

We will keep all of our JavaScript in an external file called `calendar.js`, which will
initially contain just this:

```
$(document).ready(function() {
  $('#calendar_wrapper').weekCalendar({
    'height':function($calendar){
      return $('#calendar_wrapper')[0].offsetHeight;
    }
  });
});
```

This is fairly straightforward. The script will apply the widget to the `#calendar_wrapper` element, and the widget's height will be set to that of the wrapper element.

Even with this tiny bit of code, we already have a good-looking calendar, and when you drag your mouse cursor around it, you'll see that events are created as you lift the mouse up:

It looks good, but it doesn't do anything yet. The events are temporary, and will vanish as soon as you change the week or reload the page. In order to make them permanent, we need to send details of the events to the server and save them there.

Creating an event

What we need to do is to have the client save the event on the server when it is created.

In this chapter, we'll use PHP sessions to save the data for the sake of simplicity.

> **Sessions** are chunks of data, which are kept on the server side and are related to the cookie or `PHPSESSID` parameter that the client uses to access that session. We will use sessions in these examples because they do not need as much setup as databases.

For your own projects, you should adapt the PHP side in order to connect to a database instead.

If you are using this chapter to create a full application, you will obviously want to use something more permanent than sessions, in which case the PHP code should be adapted such that all references to sessions are replaced with database references instead. This is beyond the scope of this book, but as you are a PHP developer, you probably do this everyday anyway!

When the event has been created, we want a modal dialog to appear and ask for more details. In this test case, we'll add a text area for further details, which allows for more data than would appear in the small visible area in the calendar itself.

A **modal dialog** is a "pop up" that appears and blocks all other actions on the page until it has been taken care of. It's useful in cases where the answer to a question must be known before a script can carry on with its work.

Now, let's create an event and add it to our calendar.

Client-side code

In the `calendar.js` file, add an `eventNew` event to the `weekCalendar` call:

```
$(document).ready(function() {
  $('#calendar_wrapper').weekCalendar({
    'height':function($calendar){
      return $('#calendar_wrapper')[0].offsetHeight;
    },
    'eventNew':function(calEvent, $event) {
      calendar_new_entry(calEvent,$event);
    }
  });
});
```

When an event is created, the `calendar_new_entry` function will be called with details of the new event in the `calEvent` parameter.

Now, add the function `calendar_new_entry`:

```
function calendar_new_entry(calEvent,$event){
  var ds=calEvent.start, df=calEvent.end;
  $('<div id="calendar_new_entry_form" title="New Calendar Entry">
    event name<br />
    <input value="new event" id="calendar_new_entry_form_title" />
      <br />
    body text<br />
    <textarea style="width:400px;height:200px"
            id="calendar_new_entry_form_body">event description
```

```
        </textarea>
      </div>').appendTo($('body'));
      $("#calendar_new_entry_form").dialog({
        bgiframe: true,
        autoOpen: false,
        height: 440,
        width: 450,
        modal: true,
        buttons: {
          'Save': function() {
            var $this=$(this);
            $.getJSON('./calendar.php?action=save&id=0&start='
                +ds.getTime()/1000+'&end='+df.getTime()/1000,
              {
                'body':$('#calendar_new_entry_form_body').val(),
                'title':$('#calendar_new_entry_form_title').val()
              },
              function(ret){
                $this.dialog('close');
                $('#calendar_wrapper').weekCalendar('refresh');
                $("#calendar_new_entry_form").remove();
              }
            );
          },
          Cancel: function() {
            $event.remove();
            $(this).dialog('close');
            $("#calendar_new_entry_form").remove();
          }
        },
        close: function() {
          $('#calendar').weekCalendar('removeUnsavedEvents');
          $("#calendar_new_entry_form").remove();
        }
      });
      $("#calendar_new_entry_form").dialog('open');
    }
```

What's happening here is that a form is created and added to the body (the second line of the function), then the third line of the function creates a modal window from that form and adds some buttons to it.

Our modal dialog should look like this:

The **Save** button, when pressed, calls the server-side file `calendar.php` with the parameters needed to save the event, including the `start` and `end`, and the `title` and `body`.

When the result returns, the calendar is refreshed with the new event's data included.

When any of the buttons are clicked, we close the dialog and remove it from the page completely.

> Note how we are sending time information to the server (shown highlighted in the code we just saw). JavaScript time functions usually measure in milliseconds, but we want to send it to PHP, which generally measures time in seconds. So, we convert the value on the client so that the PHP can use the received data as it is, without needing to do anything to it. Every little helps!

Server-side code

On the server side, we want to take the new event and save it. Remember that we're doing it in sessions in this example, but you should feel free to adapt this to any other model that you wish.

Create a file called `calendar.php` and save it with this source in it:

```php
<?php
  session_start();
  if(!isset($_SESSION['calendar'])){
    $_SESSION['calendar']=array(
    'ids'=>0,
  );
```

```
}
if(isset($_REQUEST['action'])){
  switch($_REQUEST['action']){
    case 'save': // {
      $start_date=(int)$_REQUEST['start'];
      $data=array(
        'title'=>(isset($_REQUEST['title'])?$_REQUEST['title']:''),
        'body' =>(isset($_REQUEST['body'])?$_REQUEST['body']:''),
        'start'=>date('c',$start_date),
        'end'  =>date('c',(int)$_REQUEST['end'])
      );
      $id=(int)$_REQUEST['id'];
      if($id && isset($_SESSION['calendar'][$id])){
        $_SESSION['calendar'][$id]=$data;
      }
      else{
        $id= ++$_SESSION['calendar']['ids'];
        $_SESSION['calendar'][$id]=$data;
      }
      echo 1;
      exit;
// }
    }
  }
}
?>
```

In the server-side code of this project, all the requested actions are handled by a switch statement. This is done for demonstration purposes — whenever we add a new action, we simply add a new switch case. If you are using this for your own purposes, you may wish to rewrite it using functions instead of large switch cases.

The date function is used to convert the start and end parameters into ISO 8601 date format. That's the format jquery-week-calendar prefers, so we'll try to keep everything in that format.

Visually, nothing appears to happen, but the data is actually being saved.

To see what's being saved, create a new file named test.php, and use the var_dump function in it to examine the session data (view it in your browser):

```
<?php
session_start();
var_dump($_SESSION);
?>
```

Here's an example from my test machine:

```
array
  'calendar' =>
    array
      'ids' => int 3
      1 =>
        array
          'title' => string 'new event' (length=9)
          'body' => string 'event description' (length=17)
          'start' => string '2009-06-22T20:00:00+01:00' (length=25)
          'end' => string '2009-06-22T21:00:00+01:00' (length=25)
      2 =>
        array
          'title' => string 'lunch' (length=5)
          'body' => string 'yummy' (length=5)
          'start' => string '2009-06-22T13:00:00+01:00' (length=25)
          'end' => string '2009-06-22T14:00:00+01:00' (length=25)
      3 =>
        array
          'title' => string 'meeting with the client' (length=23)
          'body' => string 'demo the latest release of the software. make this good!' (length=56)
          'start' => string '2009-06-22T15:00:00+01:00' (length=25)
          'end' => string '2009-06-22T16:00:00+01:00' (length=25)
```

Loading events from the server

The next step is to load events from the server, so you can see the details of the event you've created in your browser.

Client-side code

In the JavaScript, all you need to do is to add another parameter to the startup script. Add this highlighted line to the weekCalendar call, as shown:

```
$('#calendar_wrapper').weekCalendar({
  'data':'./calendar.php?action=get_events',
  'height':function($calendar){
```

This parameter is used to tell the plugin where to check for event data.

When loaded up, the plugin will call that file (./calendar.php?action=get_events), with the extra HTML parameters start and end, both of which are measured in seconds—being the first and last second of the week respectively.

The result is expected to be a JSON string, which describes the week's events.

Server-side code

On the server side, all we need to do is to add a new case to the `switch` block:

```
case 'get_events': // {
  $arr=array();
  $start=date('c',$_REQUEST['start']);
  $end=date('c',$_REQUEST['end']);
  for($i=1;$i<$_SESSION['calendar']['ids']+1;$i++){
    if(!isset($_SESSION['calendar'][$i]))continue;
    if(strcmp($_SESSION['calendar'][$i]['start'],$end)<1
          && strcmp($_SESSION['calendar'][$i]['end'],$start)>-1){
      $d=$_SESSION['calendar'][$i];
      $arr[]=array(
        'id'    =>$i,
        'title'=>$d['title'],
        'start'=>$d['start'],
        'end'   =>$d['end']
      );
    }
  }
  echo '{"events":'.json_encode($arr).'}';
  exit;
// }
```

Note that we convert the seconds into ISO 8601 strings, and then compare all entries in the session array to see if any of them are contained in the requested time slot.

The reason we rebuild the array and don't just use it as-is is that we want to include the id of each event, and we don't want to include any fields that the plugin doesn't use.

`jquery-week-calendar` is only interested in the id, title, start, and end parameters. So, it would be a waste of bandwidth to send anything more than that.

Now we can create events and read them back.

Moving and resizing events

From the data point of view, resizing and moving are actually the same thing. When it is being recorded, the data fields that are changed are the start and end times, and nothing else. This is good, as it means we have very little extra to write.

In the widget, you resize an event by dragging its bottom border down or up, as shown:

And you move the events by dragging the top label, as shown:

Client-side code

In the `calendar.js` file, add the following new events to the `weekCalendar` call in the start-up section:

```
'eventDrop':function(calEvent, $event) {
  $.getJSON('./calendar.php?action=move',{
    'id':calEvent.id,
    'start':calEvent.start.getTime()/1000,
    'end':calEvent.end.getTime()/1000
  },null);
},
'eventResize':function(calEvent, $event) {
  $.getJSON('./calendar.php?action=move',{
    'id':calEvent.id,
    'start':calEvent.start.getTime()/1000,
    'end':calEvent.end.getTime()/1000
  },null);
},
```

Both the events are exactly the same as you would expect, because in both the cases, we are only changing the start and end times of the events.

Server-side code

In `calendar.php`, add the following to the action `switch`:

```
case 'move': // {
  $id=(int)$_REQUEST['id'];
  if(!isset($_SESSION['calendar'][$id]))exit;
  $_SESSION['calendar'][$id]['start']
    =date('c',(int)$_REQUEST['start']);
  $_SESSION['calendar'][$id]['end']
    =date('c',(int)$_REQUEST['end']);
  exit;
// }
```

Incredibly simple. Just a matter of saving the new times.

Editing events

Editing an event is slightly more complex than creating an event. We need to populate the edit form with the values of the event. However, because `jquery-week-calendar` only records the id, start and end times, and `title`, the event data does not have any of the extra fields, such as the `body` field, which are required to fill in the form.

To get around this, we wrap the form generator in an inline function, which is called after the server has been requested to supply all of the event's data.

To expand further on that, when we are asked to show the event editing form, what we need to do is to retrieve the data from the server, and send it to a callback function, which will generate the form and display it.

We will use an inline function in this case, as the code is mostly unique and is only used in this case. So, it makes sense to not create a public function out of it.

As a reminder, an **inline function** is a function that does not have a name, and is defined as a parameter to a function. In our case, we define it as the callback function for `$.getJSON` as shown next.

Client-side code

Add the following event to our previous `weekCalendar` call in `calendar.js`:

```
'eventClick':function(calEvent, $event) {
  calendar_edit_entry(calEvent,$event);
},
```

And now we create the edit form:

```
function calendar_edit_entry(calEvent,$event){
 if(!calEvent.id) return;
 var ds=calEvent.start, df=calEvent.end;
 $.getJSON('./calendar.php?action=get_event&id='
  +calEvent.id,
  function(eventdata){
   $('<div id="calendar_edit_entry_form" '
     +'title="Edit Calendar Entry">event name<br />'
     +'<input id="calendar_edit_entry_form_title" value="'
     +eventdata.title+'" /><br />body text<br />'
     +'<textarea style="width:400px;height:200px"'
     +'id="calendar_edit_entry_form_body">'
     +eventdata.body+'</textarea></div>'
   ).appendTo($('body'));
   $("#calendar_edit_entry_form").dialog({
    bgiframe: true,
    autoOpen: false,
    height: 440,
    width: 450,
    modal: true,
    buttons: {
     'Save': function() {
      var $this=$(this),start=ds.getTime()/1000,end=df.getTime()/1000;
      var body=$('#calendar_edit_entry_form_body').val();
      var title=$('#calendar_edit_entry_form_title').val();
      $.getJSON('./calendar.php?action=save&id='
        +eventdata.id+'&start='+start+'&end='+end,
        {'body':body, 'title':title},
        function(ret){
         $this.dialog('close');
         $('#calendar_wrapper').weekCalendar('refresh');
         $('#calendar_edit_entry_form').remove();
        }
      );
     },
     Cancel: function() {
```

```
      $(this).dialog('close');
      $("#calendar_edit_entry_form").remove();
    }
  },
  close: function() {
    $("#calendar_edit_entry_form").remove();
  }
});
$("#calendar_edit_entry_form").dialog('open');
});
}
```

The highlighted line indicates the beginning of the inline callback function. This looks similar to the function we wrote to create a new form, but there are enough differences between creating an event and deleting an event to warrant separate functions and forms, instead of using abstraction to combine the two.

The differences will become more obvious later in the chapter as we expand on it.

There is no visual difference between the two event forms at this point.

Note that the form creation is delayed by first using $.getJSON to ask the server for details about the selected event, which are then used by the form to fill itself with the resulting values.

Apart from the pre-filling of data, there are no large differences between the editing and saving of the data.

Server-side code

In the *Creating an event* section, we wrote PHP that already handles the saving of data that has an `id`, so there's nothing further to do there.

However, in the example in the previous section, we requested the server to provide information about a specified event. That can be handled by adding another case to the action `switch`:

```
case 'get_event': // {
  $id=(int)$_REQUEST['id'];
  if(!isset($_SESSION['calendar'][$id]))exit;
  $t=$_SESSION['calendar'][$id];
  $t['id']=$id;
  echo json_encode($t);
  exit;
// }
```

And that completes the editing of the event.

Deleting events

After creating, moving, and editing events, we might come across a case where the edit form is different from the create form. There is no reason why you would want to delete an event that has not yet been created, so there is no reason to add a **delete** button to the "Create Event" form.

We have a choice—add the **delete** button to the section at the bottom of the modal dialog, next to **Save** and **Cancel**, or add it to the body of the form itself.

I always try to add delete buttons and links where I think they cannot be hit by accident. Therefore in this case, I chose not to add it to the row of buttons at the bottom. Instead, I placed it in the form itself where there's little chance it will be clicked by accident while saving or closing the form.

And even then, if the link is clicked, there is always a secondary "Are you sure?" confirmation box.

Client-side code

In the `calendar_edit_entry` function in `calender.js`, change the beginning of the
`$.getJSON` call to this:

```
$.getJSON('./calendar.php?action=get_event&id='+calEvent.id,
  function(eventdata){
    var controls='<a href="javascript:calendar_delete_entry'
                 +'('+eventdata.id+');">[delete]</a>';
    $('<div id="calendar_edit_entry_form"
          title="Edit Calendar Entry">'
      +'<div style="float:right;text-align:right">'+controls+'</div>'
      +'event name<br />'
      +'<input id="calendar_edit_entry_form_title"
              value="'+eventdata.title+'" /><br />'
      +'body text<br />'
      +'<textarea style="width:400px;height:200px"
                 id="calendar_edit_entry_form_body">'
                 '+eventdata.body+'</textarea></div>'
      ).appendTo($('body'));
    $("#calendar_edit_entry_form").dialog({
```

The only real change is to add the `controls` variable, which lets us create more
buttons if necessary, and add that variable's contained HTML to the form.

The only control there at the moment is a **delete** link, which calls the
`calendar_delete_entry` function when clicked.

Add this function now:

```
function calendar_delete_entry(id){
  if(confirm('are you sure you want to delete this entry?')){
    $('#calendar_edit_entry_form').remove();
    $.getJSON('./calendar.php?action=delete_event&id='+id,
      function(ret){
        $('#calendar_wrapper').weekCalendar('refresh');
      }
    );
  }
}
```

Server-side code

On the server side, we add a case to handle deletes:

```
case 'delete_event': // {
  $id=(int)$_REQUEST['id'];
  unset($_SESSION['calendar'][$id]);
  echo 1;
  exit;
// }
```

All it needs to do is to unset the session variable.

With that completed, you now have the finished basics of a calendar, where you can create events, move them around, edit them, and delete them.

Walk-through of the calendar so far

We've built the basics of a weekly calendar, and before we go on to discuss recurring events, let's take the time to walk through the calendar so far with a simple example.

Let's say you have an appointment on Tuesday at 2 pm with a business partner. You add that by clicking on that time, as follows:

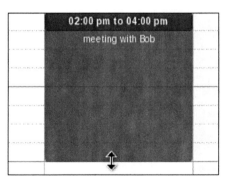

You think that the meeting will go on for about two hours, so you resize it:

Now Bob calls up early on Tuesday to say that he's not going to be able to make it, and suggests moving it to Wednesday at 1 pm. You drag the event over:

He also says that he won't be able to make it, but Sally would be there. So, you click on the event and edit the form accordingly:

Wednesday comes, and of course, something has come up on your end. You call Sally and explain that you won't be able to make it, and delete the event by clicking on the event, and then clicking on the **delete** link.

Simple and quick. What more would you want? Let's do some recurring events.

Recurring events

Sometimes you will want to have the same event automatically populated in the calendar on a recurrent basis. For example, you go to lunch every day at 1 pm, or there might be a weekly office meeting every Monday morning.

In this case, we need to come up with a way of having events recur.

This can be simple or very complex. The simplest method is what we'll demonstrate in this chapter.

The simple method involves entering a frequency (daily, monthly, and so on) and a final date, where the events stop recurring.

On the server side, when it is asked to create that recurring event, the server actually iterates over the entire requested period and adds each individual event.

This is not extremely efficient, but it's simple to write, and it's not likely that anyone would be placing years-long recurrent events on a very regular basis, so it's justifiable.

The more complex method is to only create events that are actually visible in the week you are viewing, and whenever you change the week, you check to see if there are any events that are supposed to recur that week but are not visible.

This is arguably even less efficient than the simple method, but it would allow us to be a little more flexible — for example, to leave out the final date so that the events just keep recurring.

Anyway, given that there are no major drawbacks to either method, we will choose the simpler method.

Client-side code

On the client side, recurrences are created at the same time as the recurrence of the first event. So, we edit the "Create Event" form.

In `calendar.js`, adapt the `calendar_new_entry` function by replacing the form-creation line with this:

```
var recurbox='<select id="calendar_new_entry_form_recurring">'
  +'<option value="0">non-recurring</option>'
  +'<option value="1">Daily</option>'
  +'<option value="7">Weekly</option>'
  +'</select>';
$('<div id="calendar_new_entry_form"
        title="New Calendar Entry">event name<br />'
```

```
     +'<input value="new event"
              id="calendar_new_entry_form_title" /><br />'
     +'body text<br />'
     +'<textarea style="width:400px;height:200px"
                 id="calendar_new_entry_form_body">'
       event description</textarea>'
       +recurbox+'</div>')
     .appendTo($('body'));
   $('#calendar_new_entry_form_recurring')
      .change(calendar_new_get_recurring_end);
```

This adds a select box below the body text area, requesting the user to choose a
recurring frequency (defaulting to **non-recurring**).

When the select box is changed, the function `calendar_new_get_recurring_end`
is called.

This function is used to request the final recurring date.

We could use a plain old text field, but jQuery UI includes a really cool date widget,
which allows us to request the date and have it stored in our own choice of format.

I've chosen `yyyy-mm-dd` format, as it is easy to manipulate.

Add this to `calendar.js`:

```
function calendar_new_get_recurring_end(){
  if(document.getElementById('calendar_new_recurring_end'))
    return;
  var year = new Date().getFullYear();
  var month = new Date().getMonth();
  var day = new Date().getDate();
  $('<span> until <input id="calendar_new_recurring_end"
                         value="'+year+'-'+(month+1)+'-'+day+'"
                         style="font-size:14px"
                         class="date" />'
    +'  </span>'
  ).insertAfter('#calendar_new_entry_form_recurring');
  $('.date').datepicker({
    'dateFormat':'yy-mm-dd',
    'yearRange':'-10:+50',
    'changeYear':true
  });
}
```

That creates an input field after the dropdown box, and when it is clicked, a calendar pops up:

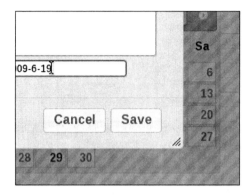

Whoops! What's happened here is that the date pop up's `z-index` is lower than the modal dialog. That can be corrected by adding this CSS line to the `<head>` section of `calendar.html`:

```
<style type="text/css">
  #ui-datepicker-div{
    z-index: 2000;
  }
</style>
```

When reloaded, the calendar now looks correct:

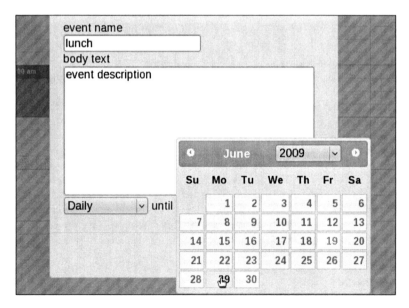

Great! Now, we just need to send the data to the server.

To do that, change the **Save** button's `$.getJSON` parameters in the `calendar_new_entry` function in `calendar.js` to these (new parameters are highlighted):

```
'body':$('#calendar_new_entry_form_body').val(),
'title':$('#calendar_new_entry_form_title').val(),
'recurring':$('#calendar_new_entry_form_recurring').val(),
'recurring_end':$('#calendar_new_recurring_end').val()
```

And we're done on the client side.

Server-side code

On the server side, the save switch case is going to change considerably, so I'll provide the entire section:

```
case 'save': // {
  $start_date=(int)$_REQUEST['start'];
  $data=array(
    'title'=>$_REQUEST['title'],
    'body' =>$_REQUEST['body'],
    'start'=>date('c',$start_date),
    'end'  =>date('c',(int)$_REQUEST['end'])
  );
  $id=(int)$_REQUEST['id'];
  if($id && isset($_SESSION['calendar'][$id])){
    if(isset($_SESSION['calendar'][$id]['recurring']))
      $data['recurring']=$_SESSION['calendar'][$id]['recurring'];
    $_SESSION['calendar'][$id]=$data;
  }
  else{
    $id=++$_SESSION['calendar']['ids'];
    $rec=(int)$_REQUEST['recurring'];
    if($rec) $data['recurring']=$id;
    $_SESSION['calendar'][$id]=$data;
    if($rec && $rec==1 || $rec==7){
      list($y,$m,$d)=explode('-',$_REQUEST['recurring_end']);
      $length=(int)$_REQUEST['end']-$start_date;
      $end_date=mktime(23,59,59,$m,$d,$y);
      $step=3600*24*$rec;
      for($j=1,$i=$start_date+$step;$i<$end_date;$j++,$i+=$step){
        $data['start']=date('c',$i);
        $data['end']=date('c',$i+$length);
        $nextid=++$_SESSION['calendar']['ids'];
```

```
            $_SESSION['calendar'][$nextid]=$data;
        }
      }
    }
    echo 1;
    exit;
  // }
```

OK. From the data point of view, we've added a single field, `recurring`, which records the first event in the series. This is needed when deleting recurring events that are not needed anymore.

When editing an existing event, all that's changed is that the recurring field (if it exists) is copied from the original before the event is overwritten with fresh data (shown highlighted).

The real action happens when creating a new event. If a recurring period is required, then the event is copied and pasted at the requested frequency from the event's first creation until the expiry date. This is figured out by counting the seconds, and incrementing as needed.

We can immediately see that recurring events work. Here's an example of a week's lunch hours created from the new recurring method:

You can shift individual events around, and even delete them, without affecting the rest.

Deleting recurring events

Finally, though, we need a way to cancel the events altogether. (Let's say lunch has become too expensive to buy.)

We will do this the same way as we did the original "Delete Event" functionality. The only difference is that this method will delete all events from the selected one onwards that were created from the same original event.

Client-side code

We are going to add a new control to the edit form, below the **delete** link.

In calendar.js, edit the calendar_new_entry function, and add the highlighted code as shown here:

```
$.getJSON('./calendar.php?action=get_event&id='+calEvent.id,
  function(eventdata){
    var controls='<a href="javascript:calendar_delete_entry('
                            +eventdata.id+');">'
                +'[delete]</a>';
    if(+eventdata.recurring)controls+='<br />'
     +'<a href="javascript:calendar_delete_recurrences('
            +eventdata.id+')">'
     +'  [stop recurring]</a>';
      $('<div id="calendar_edit_entry_form"
```

This code will add a second link, **stop recurring**, which will appear only on events that are part of a recurring sequence. (Remember that all recurring events have a "recurring" variable set to a non-zero value.)

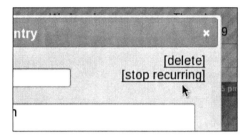

Then we need to add the referenced `calendar_delete_recurrences` function:

```
function calendar_delete_recurrences(id){
    if(confirm('This will delete this entry and all following recurrences
                of this entry\nAre you sure you want to do this?')){
      $('#calendar_edit_entry_form').remove();
      $.getJSON('./calendar.php?action=delete_event&id='
        +id+'&recurrences=1',
        function(ret){
          $('#calendar_wrapper').weekCalendar('refresh');
      });
    }
}
```

When clicked, a pop up will verify if you are certain that you want to remove the events, then will call the server with the request before refreshing.

Server-side code

On the server side, because this is basically a deletion, we will amend the existing `delete_event` case, so that it can handle both standalone and recurring events.

This is a significant change, so I'll provide the full rewrite of the case:

```
case 'delete_event': // {
  $id=(int)$_REQUEST['id'];
  if(!isset($_SESSION['calendar'][$id])) exit;
  $d=$_SESSION['calendar'][$id];
  if((int)$_REQUEST['recurrences']){
    $start=$d['start'];
    $r=$d['recurring'];
    for($i=1;$i<$_SESSION['calendar']['ids']+1;++$i){
```

```
        if(isset($_SESSION['calendar'][$i])
          && isset($_SESSION['calendar'][$i]['recurring'])
          && $_SESSION['calendar'][$i]['recurring']==$r
          && strcmp($_SESSION['calendar'][$i]['start'],$start)>0
        ){
            unset($_SESSION['calendar'][$i]);
        }
      }
    }
    unset($_SESSION['calendar'][$id]);
    echo 1;
    exit;
// }
```

What this does is to go through all recorded events, check that the event is equal to, or later than, the date of the clicked event, and ensure that the event has the same original event tagged in its recurring field.

With that done, we now have a pretty good calendar, which can handle one-off events and simple recurrences of events.

For an exercise, you could try adapting the system to use a database instead. Also, try adapting the system so that moving a recurring event will also move all the following events by the same amount.

Summary

In this chapter, we built a calendar using the `jquery-week-calendar` plugin, which can handle one-off and recurring events.

Along the way, we also got to use jQuery UI's modal dialogs, and also its `datePicker` plugin, which allows dates to be picked from a pop up calendar.

In the next chapter, we will discuss methods to manipulate images with jQuery and PHP, along with the ways to make the changes non-destructive, so that multiple manipulations can be made on the same image.

7
Image Manipulation

After uploading an image to your server, it is common that the image might be used in several ways. Instead of uploading the same image for each use, it makes sense to upload it only once, and manipulate the image online for those purposes.

The common uses could include:

- Using the image for a story, where the image is embedded in an article created using a rich text editor
- Using the image as a personal profile avatar, where the image might appear every time you make a comment on the website or create an article, or someone views your profile
- Adding the photo to an online gallery

In some cases, each of these uses can be accomplished with the same image. So, it makes sense that whatever manipulations need to be done to the image to make it suitable for the purpose, should be provided online, and the original uploaded image should not be changed so that it can be used again for other purposes.

Here's what we will be looking at in this chapter:

- Selecting an image using a simple file browser
- Manipulating the image: resizing, rotating, and cropping
- Caching the manipulated image

The most common need is for resizing. When using an image for a posted article, people tend to upload what they have, and embed it directly within their web pages, resulting in pages with a small bit of text and a 3000x2000 image artificially squashed down to 300x200.

After that is rotation. When a photo is taken, the resulting image might be sideways if the photographer turned the camera. I've seen many profile images on sites where people had uploaded images of themselves that were sideways, and the CMS did not have a way to correct this.

We'll also tackle cropping. If the focus of the image is on a small portion of it, it is not necessary to show all the uninteresting background. This is especially true when resizing, as you may end up with an image where the interesting part is so small that it is unintelligible.

Showing the list of images

There are a number of ways to select an image for manipulation. We could work solely on an image that is uploaded through a form, or use an image that is selected using the file selector tool we built in Chapter 5, *File Management*.

For the purposes of this chapter, we will use a tree view widget, which will show a selection of files that have been previously uploaded using the file manager we built, or some other way.

The jQuery UI project does not have a tree widget yet, so we will use Jörn Zaefferer's Treeview widget in the meantime, available for download at `http://bassistance.de/jquery-plugins/jquery-plugin-treeview/`.

Download the widget, and extract it into the root of your demo area.

This widget works by taking an existing `<ul>` / `<li>` HTML element tree and converting it into a more easily managed tree, similar to what you would see in a desktop's directory navigator. So, when the demo page is opened, we need to have a pre-rendered `<ul>` tree showing the directory structure of your file repository. By file repository, I mean the directories or folders that you have set aside to hold your uploaded images.

Server-side code

In this example, we will need to use a PHP file, as we're going to embed the file list directly in the HTML. So, save this file as `images.php`:

```
<html>
  <head> </head>
  <body>
    <table>
      <tr>
        <td>
```

```
            <ul id="directory_list">
<?php
require 'images_libs.php';
function get_files($base,$subdir){
 $files=array();
 foreach(new DirectoryIterator($base.$subdir) as $filename){
  if(!$filename->isDot()) $files[]=$filename.'';
 }
 natsort($files);
 return $files;
}
function show_directory($base,$subdir='/'){
 $files=get_files($base,$subdir);
 foreach($files as $filename){
  echo '<li><span title="'
    .htmlspecialchars($subdir.$filename).'" class="';
  if(is_dir($base.$subdir.$filename)){
    echo 'folder">'.htmlspecialchars($filename).'</span><ul>';
    show_directory($base,$subdir.$filename.'/');
    echo '</ul>';
  }
  else echo 'file">'.htmlspecialchars($filename).'</span>';
  echo '</li>';
 }
}
show_directory($froot);
?>
        </ul>
      </td>
      <td id="image_holder"></td>
      </tr>
      <tr>
      <td id="image_options"></td>
      <td id="image_url"></td>
      </tr>
    </table>
  </body>
</html>
```

The `images_libs.php` file needs to be created now. For now, it holds just this:

```php
<?php
$froot='/home/kae/images';
?>
```

Change the `$froot` variable to wherever you keep your own images. This will generate a `<ul>` tree, which lists all the files in that area.

Next, we need to change the look of the unordered list we've created, so that it is more appealing and usable.

What we've accomplished so far is to list all of the files located in our files repository. However, if there are a lot of files, then the list itself could be very daunting. Therefore, we need to make the list more manageable, by hiding sublists until they are actually needed.

Client-side code

Add this to the `<head>` section of the `images.php` file:

```html
<script src="../jquery.min.js"></script>
<script src="../jquery-ui.min.js"></script>
<script src="../jquery-treeview/jquery.treeview.js"></script>
<style type="text/css">
  @import '../jquery-treeview/jquery.treeview.css';

  td{vertical-align:top; border:1px solid #000;}
</style>
<script src="images.js"></script>
```

And then we need to create the new file which is referenced in the last line. Save the following as images.js:

```
$(document).ready(function(){
  $("#directory_list").treeview({
    'collapsed':true
  });
});
```

This takes the `<ul>` tree and converts it into a tree that has open and close buttons—much easier to navigate! We add the `'collapsed':true` parameter to make sure the tree starts with all the nodes closed. This makes it neater.

```
chp1
    fig_1_0.png
    fig_1_1.png
    fig_1_2.png
    fig_1_3.f /chp1/fig_1_2.png
    fig_1_4.png
    fig_1_5.png
chp2
chp3
chp4
```

Selecting an image

When an image is selected from the list, we want to show it on the right. However, as we will be manipulating the image quite a bit, we want to have the image come through a script first.

At first, there will be no manipulation at all.

Client-side code

We want the file displayed in the table cell on the right when we click on the file name. You might have noticed in the last example that every file has a title which says where in the files repository it is located.

We will make a large amendment to the images.js file, so delete all the current contents, and rewrite the file as follows:

```
function images_selectImage(imgurl){
  window.image={
    'url':imgurl,
    'effects':[]
```

```
    };
    images_showImage();
  }
  function images_showImage(){
    $('#image_holder').html(
      '<img src="images_show.php?f='+image.url+'" />'
    );
  }
  $(document).ready(function(){
    $("#directory_list").treeview({
    'collapsed':true
    });
    $('.file').click(function(){
      images_selectImage($(this).attr('title'));
    });
  });
});
```

When an image is selected, a global variable, `window.image`, is created, which holds information about it. At first, that information only contains the image's URL. Then, the image is displayed on the right by calling a file, `images_show.php` with the image URL as its parameter.

Server-side code

For now, all we need to do is to pass the file through from the repository to the client, with no manipulation along the way.

Create a file named `images_show.php` with this content:

```php
<?php
require 'images_libs.php';

if(!isset($_REQUEST['f'])) exit;
$fname=$_REQUEST['f'];
if(preg_match('#(^[^/]|^|/)\.\./#',$fname)) exit;
$ext=strtolower(preg_replace('/.*\./','',$fname));
switch($ext){
  case 'gif':
    $mime='image/gif';
    break;
  case 'jpg': case 'jpeg': case 'jpe':
    $mime='image/jpeg';
    break;
  case 'png':
    $mime='image/png';
```

```
      break;
    case 'tif': case 'tiff':
      $mime='image/tiff';
      break;
    default:
      exit; // not recognised
  }
  header('Content-type: '.$ext);
  readfile($froot.$fname);
  ?>
```

One thing to note about this is that the images do not need to be kept in a web-accessible area. They can be anywhere on the server at all, as long as the PHP can read them.

With that in place, we can now navigate and view images by clicking them.

If you are trying this out yourself, make sure that your own demo application looks like mine. Even if you don't use all of the manipulation methods in this chapter, it's still good to be able to show images from outside the web-accessible area of the web server.

Preparing your PHP

There are a number of methods to manipulate an image with PHP. Internal to PHP, there is the GD library that has been the default for a number of years. Externally, ImageMagick is a popular tool. You can read about the GD library at http://www.boutell.com/gd/, and ImageMagick can be read about at http://www.imagemagick.org/.

GD is very useful for creating graphics, such as graphs, but ImageMagick is designed from the ground up to perform manipulations on the image. It's also much faster for the things we will want to do.

As a PHP developer, you must have your own test server on which you have full control. The examples in this chapter will rely on Imagick, which is a PECL extension that lets you call ImageMagick functions from within PHP. You will probably need to install it. If you prefer to use ImageMagick through a `system()` call, or even prefer using GD, you should easily be able to convert the PHP code to do so.

To install Imagick in a Fedora or CentOS system, you need to simply type the following as root:

```
yum install php-pecl-imagick
```

Alternatively, you can get further instructions at `http://pecl.php.net/package/imagick/`.

Once the package has been installed, restart your web server. If you want to test that installation was successful, create a `test.php` file and place this in it:

```php
<?php
phpinfo();
?>
```

Visit the page in your browser, and look for a section named **imagick**. If it exists, then installation was successful.

Rotating

We'll start off the manipulation by demonstrating rotation.

Client-side code

On the client, we need to add an effects selector. For the moment, it will include **rotate** and **reset**. When **reset** is chosen, the image will be reloaded, minus the effects.

Add this line to the end of the `images_selectImage` function in the JavaScript file, `images.js`:

```
images_setupOptions();
```

That will rebuild the effect options section every time a new image is chosen. Here is the function itself, which should be added to that same file:

```
function images_setupOptions(){
    var opts=['reset','rotate'],i;
    var html='<select id="image_options_select">';
    for(i=0;i<opts.length;++i){
      html+='<option>'+opts[i]+'</option>';
    }
    html+='</select>';
    $(html)
      .change(images_changeOption)
      .appendTo($('#image_options').empty());
    $('<span id="effect_options"></span>').appendTo($('#image_options'));
}
```

You can see that the actual chooseable effects are taken from an array. To add more effects, we will simply add to that array. When an effect is chosen, we need to check what options that effect has, and show them. Add this to the images.js file as well:

```
function images_changeOption(){
    var opt=$('#image_options_select').attr('value');
    switch(opt){
      case 'reset':
        return images_selectImage(image.url);
      case 'rotate':
        return images_showRotateOptions();
    }
}
```

The **reset** option merely reloads the image, so does not need to show any editable options. The **rotate** effect, however, involves changing the image in a user-selectable way, and so needs some options defined:

```
function images_showRotateOptions(){
    var deg=0,i;
    if(image.effects.rotate) deg=image.effects.rotate;
    var html='<select id="rotate_value">';
    for(i=0;i<360;i+=90){
      html+='<option';
      if(i==deg) html+=' selected="selected"';
      html+='>'+i+'</option>';
    }
    html+='</select>';
```

```
    $(html)
      .change(images_changeRotation)
      .appendTo($('#effect_options').empty());
}
```

This shows a list of degrees: 0, 90, 180, and 270. If the number is already stored in the global `image` variable, then it will be preselected. When a different value is selected, a function is called to handle the rotation:

```
function images_changeRotation(){
    image.effects.rotate=$('#rotate_value').attr('value');
    images_showImage();
}
```

All this does is to change the global `image` variable and then redisplay the image using the new values. We will need to change the `images_showImage` function, so that it adds effect parameters to its URL, as follows:

```
function images_showImage(){
  var url='images_show.php?f='+image.url;
  for(var eff in image.effects)
    url+='&'+eff+'='+image.effects[eff];
  $('#image_holder').html('<img src="'+url+'" />');
}
```

For every effect defined in the images variable, a parameter is added to the URL. An example resulting URL might be `images_show.php?f=/chp1/test.jpg&rotate=90`.

Server-side code

On the server side, we now need to take the effects parameters and use them to change the image. If no parameters are supplied, then the image should be pushed through as normal. To do this, replace the last line of code in the `images_show.php` file (the `readfile` statement) with the following block:

```
$manipulated=0;
$effects=array('rotate');
foreach($effects as $eff)
  if(isset($_REQUEST[$eff])) $manipulated=1;

  if(!$manipulated) readfile($froot.$fname);
  else{
    $image=new Imagick($froot.$fname);

  if(isset($_REQUEST['rotate'])){
    $image->rotateImage(
      new ImagickPixel(),
```

```
        (int)$_REQUEST['rotate']
    );
    }
    echo $image;
}
```

Did you see how this works?

Unlike GD, where you need to jump through hoops to make sure you load using the right format and then convert to a true-color image before you can do anything, Imagick just loads the image and you can work on it immediately.

When the manipulation is complete, you echo it straight to the buffer.

Caching or saving the image

Image manipulation is a good thing, but it's useless if the effect is only temporary. We want to be able to manipulate the image for uses such as placing in a web page, using in a gallery, or as a profile image.

Again, there are multiple ways to do this. We could manipulate the original image, saving changes back to the image, but that's destructive. By repeatedly manipulating the same file, you risk (actually, it's much more certain than *risk*) losing information. For example, resizing something down, and then up, results in pixelated or blurred images. And cropping—well, once something is cropped, you can't recover the uncropped image.

The solution I'd recommend is to leave the original alone, and create a new image with the effects applied to it. This allows you to make multiple different versions of the same file, and also allows you to fine-tune the effects if they were a bit off the first time you did them.

To do this, I would recommend creating a second repository, separate from the first, which will contain the adapted files.

For filenames, I'd recommend using an MD5 string; they appear random, and it's exceedingly unlikely that you will create two separate images that end up with the same MD5 name.

MD5 is a mathematical manipulation, which takes a string or file, and performs a *one-way* operation on it to come up with a 32-digit hexadecimal number, which is called the **MD5 hash**.

MD5 is useful because it's extremely unlikely that any two hashes for two different strings or files will ever be the same.

We use it here and in a few other places in the book, to provide a "random" filename that is unlikely to be overwritten by another file.

So, let's do it.

Client-side code

On the client side, all we need to do is provide the permanent URL of the image.

This involves rewriting the `images_showImage` function to have it display the new permanent URL:

```
function images_showImage(){
  var params='f='+image.url;
  for(var eff in image.effects)
    params+='&'+eff+'='+image.effects[eff];
  var url='images_show.php?'+params;
  $('#image_holder').html('<img src="'+url+'" />');
  $('#image_url').html('<a href="'
    +document.location.toString()
    .replace(/[^\/]*$/,'get.php/'+params)
    +'">permanent URL</a>');
}
```

What this does is to take the parameters we were going to send to the server-side `images_show.php` file, and create a new URL from them with no question mark in it.

The reason for this is that standards-compliant browsers always reload URLs that have a question mark in them, so we need to remove the question mark. This will result in an address, such as `http://your.dom.ain/get.php/f=/chp7/IMG_0134-small.JPG&rotate=180`, which looks like just a file to a browser. You do not need `mod_rewrite` or any other such trickery to get this to work — it's built into the PHP engine itself.

Server-side code

There's a bit of shifting around that needs to take place to get this to work.

First, we need to abstract the manipulation code, so that it doesn't just manipulate the image and then print it straight to screen. We need to be able to check to see if a cached image exists of the manipulated image, and if not, create it.

Remove the entire `else` block at the end of the `images_show.php` file and replace it with this:

```
else{
  $image=get_manipulated_image($froot.$fname);
  echo $image;
}
```

In the `images_libs.php` file, we create a new function to handle all manipulations:

```
function get_manipulated_image($fname){
  $image=new Imagick($fname);
  if(isset($_REQUEST['rotate'])){
    $image->rotateImage(new ImagickPixel(),(int)$_REQUEST['rotate']);
  }
  return $image;
}
```

And then, in the `images_show.php` file, remove the section starting with the `$ext` definition and ending with the header call, and replace this entire block with this:

```
set_image_mime($fname);
```

Place the code you removed into the `images_libs.php` file as a new function:

```
function set_image_mime($fname){
  $ext=strtolower(preg_replace('/.*\./','',$fname));
  switch($ext){
    case 'gif':
```

```
      $mime='image/gif';
      break;
    case 'jpg': case 'jpeg': case 'jpe':
      $mime='image/jpeg';
      break;
    case 'png':
      $mime='image/png';
      break;
    case 'tif': case 'tiff':
      $mime='image/tiff';
      break;
    default:
      exit; // not recognized
  }
  header('Content-type: '.$mime);
  return $ext;
}
```

Note that this returns the $ext value, as that's needed by the next bit.

This action abstracts out the manipulation part and everything should still work. We now need to use that work to make a copy of the image and back it up, and serve from the backup if needed.

First, add this line to the images_libs.php file to tell the server where to store the backups:

```
$md5root='/home/kae/manipulated_images';
```

Make sure it's a directory that's writable by the server.

Now, create a file called get.php and fill it with this code:

```
<?php
require 'images_libs.php';
$params=str_replace($_SERVER['SCRIPT_NAME'].'/',
'',$_SERVER['REQUEST_URI']);
$pbits=explode('&',$params);
foreach($pbits as $pbit){
  list($name,$val)=explode('=',$pbit);
  $_REQUEST[$name]=$val;
}
if(!isset($_REQUEST['f'])) exit;
$fname=$_REQUEST['f'];
if(preg_match('#(^[^/]|^|/)\.\./#',$fname)) exit;
$ext=set_image_mime($fname);
header('Cache-Control: max-age = 2592000');
```

```
header('Expires-Active: On');
header('Expires: Fri, 1 Jan 2500 01:01:01 GMT');
header('Pragma:');
$md5name=$md5root.'/'.md5($_SERVER['REQUEST_URI']).'.png';
if(file_exists($md5name)) readfile($md5name);
else{
  $image=get_manipulated_image($froot.$fname);
  $image->writeImage($md5name);
  echo $image;
}
```

OK! What's going on here? First, we recreate the $_REQUEST parameters, based on the URL that was supplied (remember, we've replaced the ? with a /, which means there is no GET data). After that, we validate the filename, set the write MIME-type header, and then we start with the interesting part.

First, we check to see if the manipulated image already exists. If so, we just print it out. Otherwise, we create the file, and output it. What's very interesting about this is that we are now free to do what we want with the cached images directory. We can clear it out if it runs out of space, or can write a script that periodically removes the oldest image or images that have not been accessed in over a week, or whatever.

The point is, even if the cached image does not already exist, the moment it is requested by a browser it will be recreated.

Resizing

OK. Now, let's do some more manipulating tasks. Here's another simple one.

For resizing, let's keep it simple. We will show the current size in pixels, and let the client change the height or width. We will keep the aspect ratio of the original, so the image does not get skewed.

Even with that, there is still some subtle trickiness to this. The problem has to do with the order of effects. We always build up our sample image by starting with the original untouched image, but if you resize an image to 640x480 and then rotate it 90 degrees, the effect is very different from rotating 90 degrees first and then resizing to 640x480.

On the server side, we always want to carry out the effects in the same order, but on the client side, we need to be able to do them in whatever order makes sense to the user. There is no easy solution to this, so we just need to be aware of it at all times when writing.

Client-side code

To make sure that we know when an image is sideways, we change the
images_changeRotation function to make sure that this is noted in the global
image **variable.**

```
function images_changeRotation(){
  var deg=$('#rotate_value').attr('value');
  image.effects.rotate=deg;
  if(deg==90 || deg==270) image.sideways=true;
  else image.sideways=false;
  images_showImage();
}
```

Now, add rotate to the list of effects in the images_setupOptions function:

```
var opts=['reset','resize','rotate'],i;
```

And in the images_changeOption function, add a new switch case:

```
case 'resize':
return images_showResizeOptions();
```

Now, we will write the images_showResizeOptions function, keeping in mind that
rotation may skew the values:

```
function images_showResizeOptions(){
  var inps,sideways=image.sideways;
  var img=$('#image_holder img');
  var curw=img.attr('width');
  var curh=img.attr('height');
  if(!image.width || !image.height){
    image.width=curw;
    image.height=curh;
    image.aspect=curw/curh;
  }
  var inp1='<input id="image_width" size="4" value="'
   +(sideways?curh:curw)+'" />';
  var inp2='<input id="image_height" size="4" value="'
   +(sideways?curw:curh)+'" />';
  if(sideways) inps=inp2+'x'+inp1;
  else inps=inp1+'x'+inp2;
  $('<span>'+inps+'</span>')
    .appendTo($('#effect_options').empty());
  $('#effect_options input').keyup(function(){
    if(this.id=='image_width'){
      var w= +this.value;
      var h= w/image.aspect;
      document.getElementById('image_height').value=parseInt(h);
    }
```

```
    else{
      var h= +this.value;
      var w= h*image.aspect;
      document.getElementById('image_width').value=parseInt(w);
    }
  });
$('#effect_options input').change(images_resizeImage);
}
```

Due to the problem with rotation, there's a bit of trickery that goes on in there. First, we always need to keep in mind that the resize values should be the size of the image before rotation, so if we've already rotated the image on the client side, then we need to swap the numbers.

We always expect that the numbers to be shown in *width* x *height* format. So, again, if the image is sideways, we need to swap those input boxes around so that they make visual sense.

After that, we add key loggers to the input boxes. When a key is raised, we make sure that the image aspect is retained in both the boxes. When the user moves focus out of the input box (presses *Tab*, clicks, or presses *Enter*), we do the actual resizing with the images_resizeImage function:

```
function images_resizeImage(){
  var w=parseInt(document.getElementById('image_width')
    .value);
  var h=parseInt(document.getElementById('image_height')
    .value);
  if(w<1 || h<1) image.effects.resize=undefined;
  else image.effects.resize=w+'x'+h;
  images_showImage();
}
```

Note the value undefined in this. Unfortunately, for hash arrays, there is no unset in JavaScript. So, we also need to amend the images_showImage function to look out for undefined values and not add them to the parameter string. Change the parameter-building for loop to this:

```
for(var eff in image.effects){
  if(image.effects[eff]!=undefined){
    params+='&'+eff+'='+image.effects[eff];
  }
}
```

That's it for the client side. We should get a consistent URL now so that image generator always gets it the right way.

Server-side code

The server-side code is much easier. As we've done all the checks and ordering on the client side, all we need to do now is to apply what we're asked to do. In the `images_show.php` file, add `resize` to the list of effects:

```
$effects=array('rotate','resize');
```

And then, we add a new manipulation method to the `get_manipulated_image` function. It is important that this section is placed before the `rotate` method, and not after:

```
if(isset($_REQUEST['resize'])){
list($w,$h)=explode('x',$_REQUEST['resize']);
$image->resizeImage($w,$h,imagick::FILTER_CUBIC,1);
}
```

And that's it! Imagick is actually that easy to use!

Visually, a resize after a rotate looks like this:

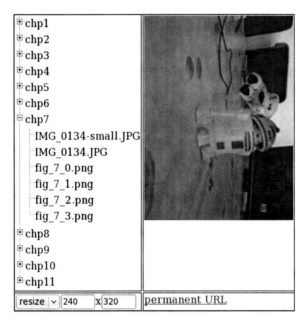

Notice how the width/height input boxes say **240x320**. Actually, because the image is rotated after the resize is done, the command that is sent to the server is to resize to 320x240 first and then rotate 90 degrees.

The **permanent URL** link is what we built in the last section. It's a link that can be used in web pages, for example, to point to the manipulated image.

Clicking on the **permanent URL** link will display the manipulated image. If there is a cached version of the image, it will be shown. If not, then a cached copy of the image will be created and then shown.

Because it is essentially a link to an image (no matter the server-side caching, and so on, that happens), it can be used in your usual HTML. For example:

```
<img src="http://play/php_and_jquery/7-6-cropping/get.php/f=/chp7/
IMG_0134-small.JPG&amp;resize=160x120&amp;crop=62,8,124,39&amp;rota
te=90" />
```

Cropping

We will handle the client side of the cropping using `Jcrop`, a plugin for jQuery written by Kelly Hallman.

Download Jcrop from `http://deepliquid.com/content/Jcrop_Download.html`, and extract so that the `Jcrop` directory is in the root of your demo directories as usual.

We still have the rotation problem to consider, so there's a little bit of thinking involved in how this is done.

Client-side code

In the `images.php` file, add these lines after the jQuery lines in the `<head>` section:

```
<script src="../Jcrop/js/jquery.Jcrop.min.js"></script>
<link rel="stylesheet" href="../Jcrop/css/jquery.Jcrop.css"
type="text/css" />
```

Now, in the `images.js` script, replace the `images_showImage` function with this:

```
function images_showImage(){
  var params='f='+image.url;
  for(var eff in image.effects){
    if(image.effects[eff]!=undefined){
      params+='&'+eff+'='+image.effects[eff];
    }
  }
  var url='images_show.php?'+params;
  $('#image_holder').empty();
```

```
$('#image_url').html('<a href="'
  +document.location.toString()
    .replace(/[^\/]*$/,'get.php/'+params)
  +'">permanent URL</a>');
var img=new Image();
img.onload=function(){
  $('#image_holder').append(this);
  var deg=0;
  if(image.effects.rotate) deg=image.effects.rotate;
  var opts={'onSelect':images_updateCropCoords};
  if(image.crop) opts.setSelect=image.crop[(360-deg)%360];
  $('#image_holder img').Jcrop(opts);
}
img.src=url;
}
```

We've had to rearrange things slightly. We want that when the image is displayed, the crop-selection tool is applied to the image, but only after the image has finished loading. I'll explain the `[(360-deg)%360]` part shortly.

We can place a dummy `images_updateCropCoords` function in for now, just to look at the basic working:

```
function images_updateCropCoords(){}
```

With the code so far, we can select an area with the mouse, but that's all—changing the image in any way will destroy the selection:

Rotating or resizing of image will cause the selection to reset.

Now, let's add the following lines in the coordinate recording mechanism:

```
function images_updateCropCoords(c){
  var x,y,x2,y2;
  var deg=0,img=$('#image_holder img');
  if(image.effects.rotate) deg=image.effects.rotate;
  var curw=img.attr('width'),curh=img.attr('height');
  var cs=[
  [c.x,c.y,c.x2,c.y2],
```

```
        [c.y,curw-c.x2,c.y2,curw-c.x],
        [curw-c.x2,curh-c.y2,curw-c.x,curh-c.y],
        [curh-c.y2,c.x,curh-c.y,c.x2]
        ];
    if(!deg) image.crop= {0:cs[0],90:cs[1],180:cs[2],270:cs[3]};
    if(deg==90) image.crop= {0:cs[1],90:cs[2],180:cs[3],270:cs[0]};
    if(deg==180) image.crop= {0:cs[2],90:cs[3],180:cs[0],270:cs[1]};
    if(deg==270) image.crop= {0:cs[3],90:cs[0],180:cs[1],270:cs[2]};
    image.effects.crop=image.crop[0];
    images_showImage();
}
```

This complex little beast is designed to take the crop coordinates, which are relative to the actual visible image, whether rotated or not, and translate those coordinates so that if you rotate the image after selecting an area, the crop coordinates will update themselves to match that. This is because the cs array is built by taking the coordinates handed in by the Jcrop plugin, and rotating them 90 degrees until we have all the four rotations covered. This is relative to the visible image's rotation, not the original image.

Then, we need to record the numbers in the global image variable, so that we can reuse them if the image is rotated. To do that, we first rotate them all back relative to the current image rotation, so that they are in the proper order — we want the array to start with degree 0.

Now, the [(360-deg)%360] bit. When the image is displayed, it may already be rotated, in which case we want the crop selection also to start rotating. Because we stored the coordinates by turning the crop around to 0 degrees, we need to reverse this when choosing the new coordinates. So, we do that by subtracting the current image rotation from 360, modulus it by 360 (using clock math), so that we end up with 0, 90, 180, or 270, and use the values in the array corresponding to that.

And finally, the image is re-shown. This is done so that the permanent URL is updated with the new crop coordinates.

Complex, maybe, but now I've done it, so you don't have to.

What it ends with is that the image can now be rotated, and the crop selection will rotate with it.

Server side

OK. Now, with the crop selection and rotation of the selection done, we need to do the actual cropping of the image.

Let's say the image we have is this:

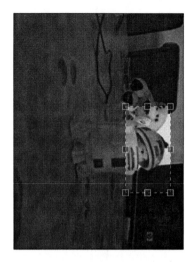

In the image editor, it would be silly to actually show the cropped image, as then you wouldn't be able to adjust the crop selection outwards. Instead, we only show the cropped version in the end result—the image that is displayed by viewing the permanent URL.

The permanent URL in this case is similar to this:

```
/get.php/f=/chp7/IMG_0134-small.JPG&crop=127,19,243,81&rotate=90
```

Note that even though the image is rotated, the crop coordinates are as if the image was not. That was the point of the last section—we will first crop on the server side before performing the rotate.

So, in the images_libs.php file, add this manipulation method after the resize and before the rotate:

```
if(isset($_REQUEST['crop'])){
  list($x1,$y1,$x2,$y2)=explode(',',$_REQUEST['crop']);
  $image->cropImage($x2-$x1,$y2-$y1,$x1,$y1);
}
```

That's it! Now, we can see the end result by viewing the permanent URL:

And in order to make sure the crop does not happen for our main editing image, we remove the crop parameter from the REQUEST array in the images_show.php file by adding this line just before the get_manipulated_image statement:

```
if(isset($_REQUEST['crop'])) unset($_REQUEST['crop']);
```

And we're done. We now have a simple editor, which can handle the most commonly needed file manipulation tricks, and is also non-destructive — we can make as many different versions of the original image as we want.

Summary

In this chapter, we looked at how to non-destructively manipulate an uploaded image.

We also discussed how to make the image cacheable, and the problems inherent in the order in which effects are carried out.

If you wish to see what other fantastic image manipulation can be done with JavaScript, I would recommend you to look at the website http://www.pixastic.com/, which includes a jQuery plugin to allow you to do some client-side image manipulation purely within the browser.

In the next chapter, we will look at a few uses of drag and drop, including sorting lists, dragging between lists, and hierarchical sorting.

8
Drag and Drop

Drag and drop is a very natural method of manipulation for web users. Web users tend to have one hand on the mouse most of the time anyway, so dragging an item around is quicker and easier than using the keyboard or laboriously clicking away until the item is in the right place.

In this chapter, we'll look at a few different ways in which drag and drop can be used to enhance your content management system, including sorting simple lists, dragging between lists, and tree-based lists.

There are other forms of drag and drop available in jQuery's UI project, but we will concentrate on the `sortable` method, as it is the easiest to use and versatile enough to be used for almost anything that you would want drag/drop for.

In this chapter, we will discuss how to use jQuery and PHP for accomplishing the following tasks:

- Sorting simple lists
- Moving items from one list to another
- Implementing nested sorts

Sorting simple lists

A very common use for drag and drop in content management systems is to sort lists. An important example of a list is the navigation of the site.

In this example, we'll look at how to sort a one-dimensional array—a very simple list that is not hierarchical.

Client-side code

To avoid the page flickering, which would happen if we obtained the list order after the page loaded and then displayed it, it makes sense to print out the HTML for the list in the right order in the first place. To do this, the file needs to be rendered with PHP.

Here's an example of what we want the browser to start with—save it as `sorting-lists.php`:

```
<html>
  <head>
    <script src="../jquery.min.js"></script>
    <script src="../jquery-ui.min.js"></script>
    <script src="sorting-lists.js"></script>
    <link rel="stylesheet" type="text/css"
          href="../jquery-ui.css" />
    <style type="text/css">
      ul{ list-style:none; width:160px; margin:0; padding:0; }
      li{ height:18px; padding: 2px 4px; margin:2px;
          border:1px solid #666; }
      li span{ float:left; }
    </style>
  </head>
  <body>
    <p>Drag the items to sort them. If you reload the page, they
      will retain that order.</p>
    <ul id="menu_items">
      <li id="menu_item_Home">Home</li>
      <li id="menu_item_About Us">About Us</li>
      <li id="menu_item_Contact Us">Contact Us</li>
      <li id="menu_item_Products">Products</li>
    </ul>
  </body>
</html>
```

This renders a simple list like this:

Home
About Us
Contact Us
Products

The only part there that needs to be dynamic is the `menu_items` list. I'll explain how to handle this in a moment, after we look at the JavaScript.

Create a file named `sorting-lists.js` and place this in it:

```
$(document).ready(function(){
  $('#menu_items').sortable({
    'stop':sl_recordChange
  }).disableSelection();
  $('<span class="ui-icon ui-icon-arrowthick-2-n-s"></span>')
    .prependTo($('#menu_items > li'));
});
```

In the `$(document).ready` function, the first line makes the menu array sortable, and tells jQuery to alert the `sl_recordChange` function when the sorting is completed. The `sortable` function adds drag/drop handlers to the `<li>` elements contained in the `#menu_items` list.

The `disableSelection` method is chained to the `.sortable` call because some browsers tend to select text as you're dragging it, making a big ugly blue track right across your website. The `disableSelection` function stops the browser from doing this.

Then, an icon is added to each of the menu items to indicate to the user that the menu item can be dragged up and down.

Add a dummy `sl_recordChange` function for a moment while we test it:

```
function sl_recordChange(){}
```

The menu items list now renders like this, making it more obvious that drag and drop can be used:

| ‡ Home |
| ‡ About Us |
| ‡ Contact Us |
| ‡ Products |

The sorting now actually works, but is not recorded anywhere. So, when you reload the page, it will revert to the original order:

| ‡ About Us |
| ‡ Home |
| ‡ Contact Us |
| ‡ Products |

The reason why it is not recorded is that we have not provided any programming logic to take the new order and store it.

Now, let's create the real `sl_recordChange` function. Remove the dummy function, and replace it with this:

```
function sl_recordChange(ev,d){
   var item=d.item[0];
   var p=item.parentNode;
   var ord=[];
   $('#'+p.id+' > li').each(function(){
     ord.push(this.id.replace(/menu_item_/,''));
   });
   $.get('sorting-lists-save.php?ord='+ord);
}
```

The `stop` event sends two parameters to the `sl_recordChange` function: `ev` and `d`. The first parameter holds information about the event that triggered the function. We're more interested in the second one, which holds information about the dragged object.

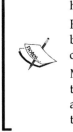

> When an event is triggered in jQuery, the engine calls the event's handler function with one or more parameters.
>
> For example, with `$('body').click(handleClick)`, when the body is clicked, `handleClick` is called with a single parameter, commonly called `ev`, which holds information about the `click` event.
>
> Many jQuery UI plugins send more than one parameter. In the case of the event handlers of `sortable`, the first parameter is the event itself, and the second parameter is commonly called `ui`. In `sortable`, this holds information about the currently dragged element.

In this case, all we need to do is to get the new order and save it. So, we get the dragged object's parent node, p, which corresponds to the `<ul>` element in the HTML, and then we look at the IDs of its direct descendants, the `<li>` elements.

Note the usage of the `each` method. It's used when you want to apply the same action to each element in an array. The array in this case is of the `<li>` elements, and the action is to add their IDs to the `ord` array.

We are using `ord` in the inline functions as if it were a global variable. In PHP, there are two scopes for variables—local and global. But in JavaScript, the scope can "bubble up".

In this case, what happens is that in the inline function we carry out an operation on a variable called `ord`. The JavaScript engine notices that `ord` was not previously defined in that function, so it bubbles up to the parent function, where we defined `ord` using the `var ord= []` statement. The engine then applies its operations to that variable.

This is the reason why you will see `var` used in JavaScript even though the language is mostly a very loosely syntaxed one. `var ord` is used to tell the engine "OK, from this point forward, we have a variable called `ord`", and the engine doesn't bubble up any further when any operation is performed on `ord`.

The `each` method strips the leading prefix, `menu_item_` from each element's ID and adds the remainder to the `ord` array.

This array is then sent to the server to save it.

Server-side code

On the server, the code couldn't be any simpler in this demo's case. Save this as `sorting-lists-save.php`:

```php
<?php
  session_start();
  if(!isset($_GET['ord'])) exit;
  $_SESSION['menu_items']=explode(',',$_GET['ord']);
?>
```

As this is a demo, we will use a session variable to record the menu order. In your own content management system, you might record it in a database instead.

Client-side code

Now, let's get back to the original HTML.

We want to now take that session-recorded list and show it in the page.

Start by starting the session engine. Add this to the top of `sorting-lists.php`:

```php
<?php
session_start();
?>
```

And now, we replace the entire `<ul>` list with a custom version.

```php
<ul id="menu_items">
<?php
  // { set up the menu_items array
  $menu_items=array('Home','About Us',
    'Contact Us','Products');
  if(isset($_SESSION['menu_items'])){
    // validate the session array
    // and replace $menu_items with it
    $tmp=$menu_items;
    $menu_items=array();
    foreach($_SESSION['menu_items'] as $item){
      if(!in_array($item,$tmp))continue;
      $menu_items[]=$item;
      unset($tmp[array_search($item,$tmp)]);
    }
    if(count($tmp)){ // session was missing an item
      foreach($tmp as $item)$menu_items[]=$item;
      $_SESSION['menu_items']=$menu_items;
    }
  }
  // }
  foreach($menu_items as $item){
    echo '<li id="menu_item_',htmlspecialchars($item),
      '">',htmlspecialchars($item),'</li>';
  }
?>
</ul>
```

Note that in the final `foreach` loop we're using the page's name in the IDs of the `<li>` elements. In your own code, you might use the primary key from your database record instead. The reason for this is that when an element is acted upon, we need to be able to tell the server-side engine what exactly was moved; and that's easiest done by using the same identifying key that the server uses itself; usually a primary key from a database.

The code could be made shorter by skipping the validation and just accepting that the session variable is correct. But, even in demos, a little bit of validation is important (just to remind the readers of the things that can go wrong).

You can apply this trick now to any one-dimensional list that needs sorting.

Sorting trees

In the last section, we discussed one-dimensional lists. However, websites are not always that simple.

When there are many pages in a website, the most common method of organization is to use a hierarchical "tree" to contain the pages.

As this will be more complex than the simple list we just did, let's start a new demo for this one.

Client-side code

We'll start off again by creating a simple HTML example:

```
<html>
  <head>
    <script src="../jquery.min.js"></script>
    <script src="../jquery-ui.min.js"></script>
    <script src="sorting-trees.js"></script>
    <style type="text/css">
      @import '../jquery-ui.css';
      ul{ list-style:none; max-width:160px; margin:0;
          padding:0; border:1px solid #000;}
      li{ padding: 2px 0 0 10px; margin:0; }
      li span{ float:left; }
    </style>
  </head>
  <body>
    <p>Drag the items to sort them. If you reload the page,
       they will retain that order.</p>
    <ul id="menu_items">
      <li id="menu_item_Home">Home</li>
      <li id="menu_item_Products">Products<ul>
        <li id="menu_item_Time Machine">Time Machine</li>
        <li id="menu_item_Transmogrifier">Transmogrifier</li>
        <li id="menu_item_Duplicator">Duplicator</li>
      </ul></li>
      <li id="menu_item_Contact Us">Contact Us</li>
      <li id="menu_item_About Us">About Us</li>
    </ul>
  </body>
</html>
```

The tree is created in this way in order to have subelements of the tree contained in new `<ul>` lists that are contained within the parent `<li>` items.

That renders like this:

```
Home
Products
    Time Machine
    Transmogrifier
    Duplicator
Contact Us
About Us
```

The last example had a border around each `<li>` element for illustrative purposes. This time, it's only around the `<ul>` elements.

The important difference between this sort and the previous one is that in this case, there are at least two separate list contexts. There is the parent list, and there is the shown **Products** list.

In order to move, say, **About Us**, into the **Products** list, we need to create a connection between the two contexts.

Luckily, jQuery makes that easy.

Here's the `sorting-trees.js` file:

```
$(document).ready(function(){
  $('#menu_items,#menu_items ul').sortable({
    'stop':sl_recordChange,
    'connectWith':['#menu_items,#menu_items ul'] ,
    'tolerance':'pointer'
  }).disableSelection();
  $('<span class="ui-icon ui-icon-arrowthick-2-n-s"></span>')
});
function sl_recordChange(){}
```

Not quite as daunting as you might have thought!

First off, the script makes the `#menu_items` child elements and the child elements of all its descendant `<ul>` elements sortable.

We have a new parameter, `connectWith`, which allows us to tell jQuery where an element can be dropped, after it's been dragged. In this case, we're saying that an element dragged from the `#menu_items` tree can be dropped in any sort context in that same tree.

> Note that the `connectWith` value `['#menu_items,#menu_items ul']` is exactly the same as the calling parameter `$('#menu_items,#menu_items ul')`.
>
> What we are telling the `sortable` plugin is that all of the levels of the nested tree are sortable, and they are all connected with each other, making it possible to drag from/to separate levels.

The `tolerance` parameter tells the `sortable` plugin when to shift a place-holder element up or down based on the position of the item you are dragging. The default value, `intersect` is not good here because of the size of the **Products** element (which has that large submenu hanging off it), so we change this value to `pointer`. The `intersect` positioning value shifts the place holders based on the size of the dragged element, but `pointer` does it based on the position of the mouse, which is more appropriate here.

With that written, you can now test it. You will see that dragging can be done into and from the submenu.

> Note that the version of jQuery UI available at the time of writing has some slight-flickering problems with this code, but the problems have been noted and code has been submitted to jQuery UI that solves this—version 1.8 should be out by the time you read this, and it will not have these problems.

Here's an image of **About Us** being dragged into the submenu:

| Home |
| Products |
| Time Machine |
| Transmogrifier |
| About Us |
| Duplicator |
| Contact Us |

Notice as well that you can drag the **Products** element around and it will take its submenu along with it:

```
Home
Contact Us

    Products
        Time Machine
        Transmogrifier
    About Us Duplicator
```

We're still missing one part of the puzzle, though — what if we want to, say, move **Transmogrifier** into a level under **Contact Us**? In order to do that, we would need to create a submenu under **Contact Us**, which does not exist at the moment.

The <ul> elements are containers for the elements, so we need to make sure that when you drop **Transmogrifier** under **Contact Us**, there is a container there to drop the element into.

This is just a matter of making sure that there is a <ul> under every single <li> in the #main_menu element, even if most of those <ul> elements are empty.

Add this to the start of the $(document).ready function:

```
$('#menu_items li').each(function(){
  if($('ul',this).length)return;
  $('<ul></ul>').appendTo(this);
});
```

And, add these parameters to the sort method call to make the drop positions more obvious:

```
'placeholder':'placeholder',
'dropOnEmpty':'false'
```

And finally, add a placeholder class to the CSS in sorting-trees.php and edit the ul definition as well:

```
ul{ list-style:none; max-width:160px; margin:0;
    padding:0; border:1px solid #000; min-height:5px;
    height:auto !important; height:5px }
.placeholder{ height:2px; background:#f00; }
```

We've changed the ul definition so that empty lists are more obvious. The doubled height declaration is because of older Internet Explorer browsers. Most browsers will use the first one, and IE6 will use the second one.

Now, reloading the page looks like this:

```
Home
Products
    Time Machine
    Transmogrifier
    Duplicator
Contact Us
About Us
```

Of course, in your own version, you can remove the borders to make it look better.

The `placeholder` class makes the target drop zone highlight in red. Here's an example with the borders removed, showing a highlighted drop zone:

```
Home
Products
    Time Machine
    Duplicator
Contact Us
    Transmogrifier
About Us
```

OK! So, now that we have a working tree, let's get to the recording of it.

The navigation tree we've built here can be considered to be a multi-dimensional array, so that's what we will build.

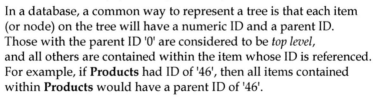

There are a number of ways to represent trees in data.

In this chapter, we will use the simplest, which is to build a multi-dimensional array, where each item in any level optionally can have a "sub" array holding further levels.

In a database, a common way to represent a tree is that each item (or node) on the tree will have a numeric ID and a parent ID. Those with the parent ID '0' are considered to be *top level*, and all others are contained within the item whose ID is referenced. For example, if **Products** had ID of '46', then all items contained within **Products** would have a parent ID of '46'.

The initial menu can be described using this array in JSON:

```
[
  ["Home",[]],
  ["Products",[
    ["Time Machine",[]],
    ["Transmogrifier",[]],
    ["Duplicator",[]]
  ]],
  ["Contact Us",[]],
  ["About Us",[]]
]
```

I've written it such that each item is an array, which contains many subitems in it.

Note that I used double quotes instead of single quotes. PHP's json_decode expects double quotes to be used for all variable names.

If you wanted to use your database's primary keys for indexing, then you might rewrite the code to generate something like this:

```
["1":["Home",0,0],
 "2":["Products",0,1],
 "3":["Time Machine",2,0],
 "4":["Transmogrifier",2,1],
 "5":["Duplicator",2,2],
 "6":["Contact Us",0,2],
 "7":["About Us",0,3]]
```

In this case, we index each item according to its key in the database, and also include data about its name, parent node, and position in its parent's list. This is not hard to do, and is mostly a PHP effort, so I'll leave that to you.

We will use the first data format for this demo.

In sorting-trees.js, replace the sl_recordChange dummy function with this real code:

```
function sl_recordChange(){
  var menu=$('#menu_items > li');
  var json='['+sl_getMenuTree(menu)+']';
  $.get('sorting-trees-save.php?ord='+json);
}
function sl_getMenuTree(menu){
  var items=[];
  menu.each(function(){
```

```
    var submenu=$('> ul > li',this);
    items.push('["'+this.id.replace(/menu_item_/,'')
      +'", ['+sl_getMenuTree(submenu)+']]');
  });
  return items.join(',');
}
```

This traverses the `#menu_items <ul>` tree recursively and adds each item to a JSON string, as already described earlier, and then sends it to `sorting-trees-save.php` for saving.

Note the use of the `>` selector operation in the CSS statements. We need to be careful to only traverse the tree one level at a time, but if we left out the `>` operators, then we might jump from the top-level `<ul>` to an `<li>` deep inside the tree.

This is because the CSS selector `ul li` will match all `<li>` elements within a `<ul>`. This includes all `<li>` elements that are held in nested `<ul>` elements within the parent one. To avoid confusion, it's important to build the JSON string very carefully and only one level at a time.

Server-side code

Again, this is a simple file. Save it as `sorting-trees-save.php`:

```php
<?php
session_start();
if(!isset($_GET['ord'])) exit;
$_SESSION['menu_items']=$_GET['ord'];
?>
```

If you were doing this for your CMS, you would have checks for security, checks to see that the sort data handles every page that it needs to, and then you'd save it to the database.

In our case, we're just using a session, for demo purposes, so it's just a matter of recording what we're given.

Now, we need to work on the `sorting-trees.php` file so that the navigation tree shown is taken from the session variable.

Start again by adding starting the session engine at the top of the file:

```php
<?php
session_start();
?>
```

And now, again, we will replace the entire `<ul>` tree:

```php
<ul id="menu_items">
<?php
  $menu_items_JSON='[["Home",[]], ["Products",[ ["Time Machine",[]],
                    ["Transmogrifier",[]], ["Duplicator",[]] ]],
                    ["Contact Us",[]], ["About Us",[]] ]';
  if(isset($_SESSION['tree_ord']))
    $menu_items_JSON=$_SESSION['tree_ord'];
  function show_items($items){
    foreach($items as $item){
      echo '<li id="menu_item_'.htmlspecialchars($item[0]).'">'
              ,htmlspecialchars($item[0]);
      if(count($item[1])){
        echo '<ul>',show_items($item[1]),'</ul>';
      }
      echo '</li>';
    }
  }
  show_items(json_decode($menu_items_JSON));
?>
</ul>
```

If you were using a database, the code would be very similar here.

What we've accomplished here is that, using very little code, we are able to drag or drop list items from one level in a nested list to any other level of the tree, and record it.

To do this without jQuery would be a very large task!

Connecting lists

We've seen how to connect lists to form a `<ul>` tree, but what if we want to just drag items from one list to another?

It's actually exactly the same. In the previous example, the lists were contained within each other, but in this case, it's a lot more obvious.

Let's say you want to create a simple emailer, which will take a list of your contacts and will email only the ones that you select.

You could do this with multi-select boxes or check boxes, but it looks nicer when you can drag the selected items into a list. You can then see the complete list a lot more clearly.

Client-side code

So first off, let's create the HTML.

Create a file called `connecting-lists.php`, and place this in it:

```php
<?php
  session_start();
  if(!isset($_SESSION['contacts']))
    $_SESSION['contacts']=array();
?>
<html>
  <head>
    <script src="../jquery.min.js"></script>
    <script src="../jquery-ui.min.js"></script>
    <script src="connecting-lists.js"></script>
    <style type="text/css">
      @import '../jquery-ui.css';
      ul{ min-height:50px; height:auto !important;
        height:50px; border:1px solid #000; margin:0; }
      td{ vertical-align:top; }
      form{ padding:0; }
    </style>
  </head>
  <body>
    <table>
      <tr><th>Contacts</th><th>People to Email</th></tr>
      <tr>
        <td>
        <ul id="contacts" class="email_contacts">
        <?php
          $contacts=array( '1'=>'Albertus Ackleton',
                           '2'=>'Bob Burry',
                           '3'=>'Cora Cuddlesby',
                           '4'=>'Derren Drufus');
          foreach($contacts as $key=>$val){
            if(!isset($_SESSION['contacts'][$key])){
            echo '<li><input type="hidden"
                         name="contacts[', $key,']"/>',
                             htmlspecialchars($val),'</li>';
            }
          }
        ?>
        </ul>
        </td>
```

```
        <td><form method="post">
          <ul id="to_email" class="email_contacts">
          <?php
            foreach($contacts as $key=>$val){
              if(isset($_SESSION['contacts'][$key])){
                echo '<li><input type="hidden"
                                  name="contacts[', $key,']" />',
                                  htmlspecialchars($val),'</li>';
              }
            }
          ?>
          </ul>
          <strong>Message</strong><br />
          <textarea name="message"></textarea><br />
          <input type="submit" name="action" value="send email" />
        </form></td>
      </tr>
    </table>
  </body>
</html>
```

An important thing to note here is that we are moving the `<li>` elements that contain hidden input boxes. This means we can drag them into a form and submit that form.

This is important because in the previous examples, we've been saving the information "on the fly", but in a case such as this, where there are potentially hundreds of contacts, you do not want all of that information to be saved every time a tiny change is made.

Here is `connecting-lists.js`:

```
$(document).ready(function(){
  $('.email_contacts').sortable({
    'connectWith':['.email_contacts']
  });
});
```

In the previous examples, we used the ID of top-level `<ul>` element to identify what lists should be sorted, but in this case, we are using class names. The reason is that in a tree-based navigation menu, there could be many submenus. So, the corresponding HTML would be very large if we needed to include class names in every `<ul>` of the tree.

In this case, we can link the two lists together semantically by using the class `email_contacts` (after all, that's what they both are), and can then use that class name to identify the elements to the `sortable` method.

This is immediately usable:

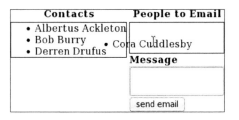

Server-side code

The only server-side code we need to write here is to send the email and to record the contents of the **People to Email** list.

We can do this in the top section of `connecting-lists.php`, just before the `?>`:

```
if(isset($_POST['contacts']))
  $_SESSION['contacts']=$_POST['contacts'];
/*
pretend your email-sending routine is here
*/
```

In this example, I've used numbers to identify the contacts, so you should be able to convert it easily to use for your own databases if you want.

Summary

In this chapter, we looked at a few ways that drag and drop can be used to improve the usability of your content management system.

All the examples in this chapter used `<ul>` lists. With creative thinking, this kind of list can be used for all sorts of purposes.

We used `<ul>` lists in this chapter to sort a simple list, to build a navigation tree, and to select contacts to send emails.

In the next chapter, we will build a very large data table and discuss how to navigate and search it using jQuery and Ajax.

9
Data Tables

From time to time, you will want to show data in your website and allow the data to be sorted and searched.

It always impresses me that whenever I need to do anything with jQuery, there are usually plugins available, which are exactly or close to what I need.

In this chapter, we will look at:

- How to install and use the `DataTables` plugin
- How to load data pages on request from the server
- Searching and ordering the data

The `DataTables` plugin allows sorting, filtering, and pagination on your data.

Here's an example screen from the project we will build in this chapter. The data is from a database of cities of the world, filtered to find out if there is any place called **nowhere** in the world:

Show 10 ∨ entries			Search:
			nowhere
Country ⇕	**City** ▼	**Latitude** ⇕	**Longitude** ⇕
us	nowhere	35.1592	-98.4419
Showing 1 to 1 of 1 entries (filtered from 2673764 total entries)			◄ ►

Get your copy of `DataTables` from `http://www.datatables.net/`, and extract it into the directory `datatables`, which is in the same directory as the `jquery.min.js` file.

What the `DataTables` plugin does is take a large table, paginate it, and allow the columns to be ordered, and the cells to be filtered.

Setting up DataTables

Setting up `DataTables` involves setting up a table so that it has distinct `<thead>` and `<tbody>` sections, and then simply running `dataTable()` on it.

As a reminder, tables in HTML have a header and a body. The HTML elements `<thead>` and `<tbody>` are optional according to the specifications, but the `DataTables` plugin requires that you put them in, so that it knows what to work with.

These elements may not be familiar to you, as they are usually not necessary when you are writing your web pages and most people leave them out, but `DataTables` needs to know what area of the table to turn into a *navigation bar*, and which area will contain the data, so you need to include them.

Client-side code

The first example in this chapter is purely a client-side one. We will provide the data in the same page that is demonstrating the table.

Copy the following code into a file in a new demo directory and name it `tables.html`:

```html
<html>
  <head>
    <script src="../jquery.min.js"></script>
    <script src="../datatables/media/js/jquery.dataTables.js">
    </script>
    <style type="text/css">
      @import "../datatables/media/css/demo_table.css";</style>
    <script>
      $(document).ready(function(){
        $('#the_table').dataTable();
      });
    </script>
  </head>
  <body>
    <div style="width:500px">
      <table id="the_table">
        <thead>
          <tr>
            <th>Artist / Band</th><th>Album</th><th>Song</th>
          </tr>
        </thead>
        <tbody>
          <tr><td>Muse</td>
              <td>Absolution</td>
              <td>Sing for Absolution</td>
          </tr>
          <tr><td>Primus</td>
```

```
        <td>Sailing The Seas Of Cheese</td>
        <td>Tommy the Cat</td>
      </tr>
      <tr><td>Nine Inch Nails</td>
          <td>Pretty Hate Machine</td>
          <td>Something I Can Never Have</td>
      </tr>
      <tr><td>Horslips</td>
        <td>The Táin</td>
        <td>Dearg Doom</td>
      </tr>
      <tr><td>Muse</td>
          <td>Absolution</td>
          <td>Hysteria</td>
      </tr>
      <tr><td>Alice In Chains</td>
        <td>Dirt</td>
        <td>Rain When I Die</td>
      </tr>
      <!-- PLACE MORE SONGS HERE -->
    </tbody>
  </table>
 </div>
 </body>
</html>
```

When this is viewed in the browser, we immediately have a working data table:

Show 10 ∨ entries		Search:
Artist / Band▲	**Album** ⬍	**Song** ⬍
Alice In Chains	Dirt	Rain When I Die
Alice In Chains	Dirt	Rooster
Baby Chaos	Love Your Self Abuse	Mental Bruising For Beginners
Baby Chaos	Love Your Self Abuse	She's In Pain
Einstürzende Neubauten	Tabula Rasa	Die Interimsliebenden
Einstürzende Neubauten	Tabula Rasa	Blume
Horslips	The Táin	Dearg Doom
Horslips	The Táin	Faster Than The Hound
Muse	Absolution	Sing for Absolution
Muse	Absolution	Hysteria
Showing 1 to 10 of 14 entries		◀ ▶

Note that the rows are in alphabetical order according to **Artist/Band**. `DataTables` automatically sorts your data initially based on the first column.

The HTML provided has a `<div>` wrapper around the table, set to a fixed width. The reason for this is that the **Search** box at the top and the pagination buttons at the bottom are floated to the right, outside the HTML table. The `<div>` wrapper is provided to try to keep them at the same width as the table.

There are 14 entries in the HTML, but only 10 of them are shown here. Clicking the arrow on the right side at the bottom-right pagination area loads up the next page:

Artist / Band ▲	Album	Song
Nine Inch Nails	Pretty Hate Machine	Something I Can Never Have
Nine Inch Nails	Pretty Hate Machine	Head Like A Hole
Primus	Sailing The Seas Of Cheese	Tommy the Cat
Primus	Sailing The Seas Of Cheese	Is It Luck?

Show `10 ▾` entries   Search:

Showing 11 to 14 of 14 entries   ◀ ▶

And finally, we also have the ability to sort by column and search all data:

Show `10 ▾` entries   Search: horslips

Artist / Band	Album	Song ▾
Horslips	The Táin	Faster Than The Hound
Horslips	The Táin	Dearg Doom

Showing 1 to 2 of 2 entries (filtered from 14 total entries)   ◀ ▶

In this screenshot, we have the data filtered by the word **horslips**, and have ordered **Song** in descending order by clicking the header twice.

With just this example, you can probably manage quite a few of your lower-bandwidth information tables. By this, I mean that you could run the `DataTables` plugin on complete tables of a few hundred rows. Beyond that, the bandwidth and memory usage would start affecting your reader's experience. In that case, it's time to go on to the next section and learn how to serve the data on demand using jQuery and Ajax.

As an example of usage, a user list might reasonably be printed entirely to the page and then converted using the `DataTable` plugin because, for smaller sites, the user list might only be a few tens of rows and thus, serving it over Ajax may be overkill. It is more likely, though, that the kind of information that you would really want this applied to is part of a much larger data set, which is where the rest of the chapter comes in!

Getting data from the server

The rest of the chapter will build up a sample application, which is a search application for cities of the world.

This example will need a database, and a large data set. I chose a list of city names and their spelling variants as my data set. You can get a list of this type online by searching.

The exact point at which you decide a data set is large enough to require it to be converted to serve over Ajax, instead of being printed fully to the HTML source, depends on a few factors, which are mostly subjective.

A quick test is: if you only ever need to read a few pages of the data, yet there are many pages in the source and the HTML is slow to load, then it's time to convert.

The database I'm using in the example is MySQL (`http://www.mysql.com/`). It is trivial to convert the example to use any other database, such as PostgreSQL or SQLite.

For your use, here is a short list of large data sets:

- `http://wordlist.sourceforge.net/` — Links to collections of words.
- `http://www.gutenberg.org/wiki/Gutenberg:Offline_Catalogs` — A list of books placed online by Project Gutenburg.
- `http://www.world-gazetteer.com/wg.php?men=stdl` — A list of all the cities in the world, including populations.

The reason I chose a city name list is that I wanted to provide a realistic large example of when you would use this.

In your own applications, you might also use the `DataTables` plugin to manage large lists of products, objects such as pages or images, and anything else that can be listed in tabular form and might be very large.

The city list I found has over two million variants in it, so it is an extreme example of how to set up a searchable table.

It's also a perfect example of why the Ajax capabilities of the DataTables project are important. Just to see the result, I exported all the entries into an HTML table, and the file size was 179 MB. Obviously, too large for a web page.

So, let's find out how to break the information into chunks and load it only as needed.

Client-side code

On the client side, we do not need to provide placeholder data. Simply print out the table, leaving the `<tbody>` section blank, and let `DataTables` retrieve the data from the server.

We're starting a new project here, so create a new directory in your demos section and save the following into it as `tables.html`:

```html
<html>
  <head>
    <script src="../jquery.min.js"></script>
    <script src="../datatables/media/js/jquery.dataTables.js">
    </script>
    <style type="text/css">
      @import "../datatables/media/css/demo_table.css";
      table{width:100%}
    </style>
    <script>
      $(document).ready(function(){
        $('#the_table').dataTable({
          'sAjaxSource':'get_data.php'
        });
      });
    </script>
  </head>
  <body>
    <div style="width:500px">
      <table id="the_table">
        <thead>
          <tr>
            <th>Country</th>
            <th>City</th>
            <th>Latitude</th>
            <th>Longitude</th>
          </tr>
```

```
            </thead>
            <tbody>
            </tbody>
          </table>
        </div>
      </body>
  </html>
```

In this example, we've added a parameter to the `.dataTable` call, sAjaxSource, which is the URL of the script that will provide the data (the file will be named get_data.php).

Server-side code

On the server side, we will start off by providing the first ten rows from the database.

DataTables expects the data to be returned as a two-dimensional array named aaData.

In my own database, I've created a table like this:

```
CREATE TABLE `cities` (
  `ccode` char(2) DEFAULT NULL,
  `city` varchar(87) DEFAULT NULL,
  `longitude` float DEFAULT NULL,
  `latitude` float DEFAULT NULL,
  KEY `city` (`city`(5))
) ENGINE=MyISAM DEFAULT CHARSET=utf8
```

Most of the searching will be done on city names, so I've indexed city.

Initially, let's just extract the first page of information. Create a file called get_data.php and save it in the same directory as tables.html:

```
<?php
// { initialise variables
  $amt=10;
  $start=0;
// }
// { connect to database
  function dbRow($sql){
    $q=mysql_query($sql);
    $r=mysql_fetch_array($q);
    return $r;
  }
  function dbAll($sql){
```

```php
        $q=mysql_query($sql);
        while($r=mysql_fetch_array($q))$rs[]=$r;
        return $rs;
    }
  mysql_connect('localhost','username','password');
  mysql_select_db('phpandjquery');
// }
// { count existing records
  $r=dbRow('select count(ccode) as c from cities');
  $total_records=$r['c'];
// }
// { start displaying records
  echo '{"iTotalRecords":'.$total_records.',
        "iTotalDisplayRecords":'.$total_records.',
        "aaData":[';
  $rs=dbAll("select ccode,city,longitude,latitude from cities
            order by ccode,city limit $start,$amt");
  $f=0;
  foreach($rs as $r){
    if($f++) echo ',';
    echo '["',$r['ccode'],'",
          "',addslashes($r['city']),'",
          "',$r['longitude'],'",
          "',$r['latitude'],'"]';
  }
echo ']}';
// }
```

In a nutshell, what happens is that the script counts how many cities are there in total, and then returns that count along with the first ten entries to the client browser using JSON as the transport.

A sample JSON result for this (formatted for easier reading) is this:

```json
{
  "iTotalRecords":2673762,
  "iTotalDisplayRecords":2673762,
  "aaData":[
    ["ad","aixas","42.4833","1.46667"],
    ["ad","aixirivali","42.4667","1.5"],
    ["ad","aixirivall","42.4667","1.5"]
  /* and 7 more... */
  ]
}
```

The three parameters in this JSON array are:

- `iTotalRecords` is the total number of records in the database
- `iTotalDisplayRecords` is the total number after filtering (explained later)
- `aaData` is a two-dimensional array of data that corresponds to the rows and columns of the shown table

For the moment, `iTotalRecords` is equal to `iTotalDisplayRecords`. Later in the chapter, we'll see how this would change.

Country ▲	City ⬍	Latitude ⬍	Longitude ⬍
ad	aixas	42.4833	1.46667
ad	aixirivali	42.4667	1.5
ad	aixirivall	42.4667	1.5
ad	aixirvall	42.4667	1.5
ad	aixovall	42.4667	1.48333
ad	andorra	42.5	1.51667
ad	andorra la vella	42.5	1.51667
ad	andorra-vieille	42.5	1.51667
ad	andorre	42.5	1.51667
ad	andorre-la-vieille	42.5	1.51667

Show 10 ⌄ entries   Search:

Showing 1 to 10 of 2673762 entries

If you have done like I did, and have installed a very large database, you'll see the first ten entries of the table appear in the browser several seconds after the page opens.

This is because it is much slower to build a list of items from a database than it is to just read the list directly from a file.

We'll address that now, and will come back to pagination, ordering, and searches afterwards.

Caching your database queries

In any large database, it is important to cache your queries. Database calls can be quite expensive, even after careful tuning.

In the database that I set up for this, there are over two million rows, and queries can take seconds to complete (tens of seconds if no indexing is done).

While modern databases do include caching engines for popular queries, it is much better to simply open and read a file that contains cached information that translates to "There are 2673762 rows in this database" than to have the database actually count the rows.

We will create a very simple caching mechanism that takes the requested query, encodes the query to a string using MD5, then returns the cached query if it exists, and creates the cache if not. Remember, MD5 returns a pseudo-random string of characters that can be used to save a cache with a unique name.

A nice thing about cities and countries is that the data does not change very quickly. So, it would not be necessary to clear the cache all that often—after a few hundred queries through it, it should be quite fast, as the most common searches will be cached quickly, and non-cached searches will increasingly only be for rarer requests.

Server-side code

So, let's add the caching functions. Add this to the top of get_data.php:

```
// { caching functions
function cache_load($md5){
  if(file_exists('cache/'.$md5)){
     return json_decode(file_get_contents('cache/'.$md5), true);
  }
  return false;
}
function cache_save($md5,$vals){
  file_put_contents('cache/'.$md5, json_encode($vals));
}
// }
```

These functions read and write from a directory named cache contained in the same directory as the file itself. Create the directory and make sure it is writable by the server.

The reason I use json_encode instead of serialize is that if I ever want to pass the data directly back to jQuery without re-encoding it, then JSON is perfect. With serialize, I would need to decode it in PHP, then re-encode as JSON before sending it on.

Now, we need to change the database querying functions so that they read from the cache if possible. Change the two functions to:

```
function dbRow($sql){
  $r=cache_load(md5($sql));
  if($r===false){
    $q=mysql_query($sql);
    $r=mysql_fetch_array($q);
    cache_save(md5($sql),$r);
  }
  return $r;
}
function dbAll($sql){
  $rs=cache_load(md5($sql));
  if($rs===false){
    $rs=array();
    $q=mysql_query($sql);
    while($r=mysql_fetch_array($q)) $rs[]=$r;
    cache_save(md5($sql),$rs);
  }
  return $rs;
}
```

Note that this caches all queries—if you are using this in a project where the data is more volatile, then you will want to change the caching method to only cache data you are sure is likely to be static, and to allow for easy clearing of the cache in case of data changing.

Before we carry on, you should verify for yourself that there is a marked improvement in the speed. Load up the page a few times first using the non-cached version, and time it, and then load up the cached version a few times. On very large data sets, the speed difference should be very obvious.

If you overwrote your cache, you can emulate this, by manually removing the server's cache after each page load.

Pagination through Ajax

OK, we've got some data from the server, and we've made the query run quickly, so now let's get onto pagination.

To get pagination working, we need to perform the data sorting on the server instead of the browser. It is not possible for the sorting to be done on the client side because in order to do that, the DataTables plugin must have all of the sortable data in memory.

Client-side code

In table.html, change the dataTable call to this:

```
$('#the_table').dataTable({
  'bProcessing':true,
  'bServerSide':true,
  'sAjaxSource':'get_data.php'
});
```

The bServerSide parameter tells DataTables to do all the processing on the server—that is, don't do any sorting or searching locally, as the browser does not have the information it needs to do this.

The bProcessing parameter adds a small text message, **processing**, to the screen when it's retrieving the information from the server. You can use CSS to make this message more obvious if you want.

Server-side code

If you load up table.html in your browser now and look at the query that's sent (using a debugging tool such as Firebug or TamperData), you will see something like this:

```
http://your.site/9-2-loading-dynamically/get_data.php?sEcho=1&iColumns
=4&sColumns=&iDisplayStart=0&iDisplayLength=10&sSearch=&bEscapeRegex=t
rue&sSearch_0=&bEscapeRegex_0=true&sSearch_1=&bEscapeRegex_1=true&sSea
rch_2=&bEscapeRegex_2=true&sSearch_3=&bEscapeRegex_3=true&iSortingCols
=1&iSortCol_0=0&iSortDir_0=asc
```

Quite a lot in there!

Broken apart, this URL has the following parameters:

- sEcho: Internal variable.
- iColumns: Number of columns being displayed.
- sColumns: List of column names.
- iDisplayStart: Where to paginate from.
- iDisplayLength: Number of rows that are visible.
- sSearch: String to search globally for.
- bEscapeRegex: Whether search is a regular expression.
- sSearch_*(int)*: Column-specific search (one each for each column).

- `bEscapeRegex_` *(int)*: Whether or not the column-specific searches are regular expression objects.

- `iSortingCols`: Number of columns to sort by.

- `iSortDir`: Direction to sort in.

The interesting parts for us at the moment are `iDisplayLength` and `iDisplayStart`, which tell us how many rows to send back, and where in the results to start. Essentially, they're the numbers to feed into MySQL's limit clause.

In the earlier example URL, we're starting at the beginning, at `iDisplayStart=0`, and reading 10 values; `iDisplayLength=10`, which is the default for `DataTables`.

In `get_data.php`, we already have an "initialize variables" section, with values hardcoded.

Replace that section with this code:

```
// { initialize variables
// { amount of records to show
$amt=10;
if(isset($_REQUEST['iDisplayLength'])){
  $amt=(int)$_REQUEST['iDisplayLength'];
  if($amt>100 || $amt<10)$amt=10;
}
// }
// { where to start showing the records from
$start=0;
if(isset($_REQUEST['iDisplayStart'])){
  $start=(int)$_REQUEST['iDisplayStart'];
  if($start<0) $start=0;
}
// }
// }
```

That just reads in what's requested, and makes sure the numbers are sane.

We already wrote the queries in such a way that they accept variable starts and row numbers. So, that's basically it—you can now load the next page, change the visible number, and so on.

Next, we need to fix it so that column sorting is obeyed.

Sorting by column

In the URL string shown in the last section, there are a few parameters to do with sorting:

- iSortingCols: This defines the number of columns that we are sorting. (We'll stick with just one for this chapter.)

- iSortCol_0: This defines the first column to sort. The value is numerical, starting with 0, and corresponds to what columns are displayed in the table, not the fields in the database.

- iSortDir_0: This defines the direction the column should be sorted in. Handily, this value is either asc or desc, which we can plug directly into the query.

To make use of the numerical nature of iSortCol_0, we will add an array of column names to get_data.php. Add it to the "initialize variables" block:

```
$cols=array('ccode','city','longitude','latitude');
```

And then, we will generate MySQL's order by clause's information by adding the following just below this line:

```
// { sort by
$scol=0;
if(isset($_REQUEST['iSortCol_0'])){
    $scol=(int)$_REQUEST['iSortCol_0'];
    if($scol>3 || $scol<0) $scol=0;
}
$sdir='asc';
if(isset($_REQUEST['iSortDir_0'])){
    if($_REQUEST['iSortDir_0']!='asc') $sdir='desc';
}
$scol_name=$cols[$scol];
// }
```

Again, just a little sanitizing goes into it. The values asc and desc are sanitized by recognising that there are only two possible values. If it's not one, it must be the other.

And the main query is then amended to include order information:

```
$rs=dbAll("select ccode,city,longitude,latitude
        from cities
        order by $scol_name $sdir limit $start,$amt");
```

You can now do interesting queries, such as finding the most northern cities in the world by sorting in descending order by latitude:

Country	City	Latitude	Longitude
ca	alert	82.4833	-62.25
ca	discovery harbor	81.7167	-64.7167
ca	fort conger	81.7167	-64.7167
gl	nord	81.7167	-17.8
ca	eureka	80.2167	-86.1833
gl	nunatame	80	-66
gl	nunatami	80	-66
sj	neu-aalesund	78.9333	11.95
sj	new aalesund	78.9333	11.95
sj	ny-alesund	78.9333	11.95

Show `10` entries   Search:

Showing 1 to 10 of 2673762 entries

Canada, Greenland, and Svalbard (part of Norway) — brr!

Notice that some of the entries are repeated. This is because my sample database includes alternative spellings as well. Numerous separate spellings, and Ny-Ålesund only has 40 inhabitants!

Filtering

Of course, no data table is complete without filtering. There's no point having a few million results if you can't narrow it down to a manageable level.

The URL string we're working with includes a number of sSearch parameters: the sSearch parameter itself and an sSearch_0/1/2/3 parameter for each of the table columns. We will only use the main sSearch in this chapter's example.

In our example, we will take the string we're given, and match it against the beginning of the city name field, and if there are exactly two letters, will also match it against the country.

Server-side code

First, we need to set up MySQL's where clause. Add this to the "initialize variables" section of get_data.php:

```
// { search
$search_sql='';
if(isset($_REQUEST['sSearch']) && ''!=$_REQUEST['sSearch']){
```

```
$stext=addslashes($_REQUEST['sSearch']);
$search_sql='where ';
if(strlen($stext)==2) $search_sql.="ccode='$stext' or ";
                      $search_sql.="city like '$stext%'";
}
// }
```

This section builds up a `$search_sql` string if needed, which compares against `city` and optionally also against the country code.

Now, we can set up the `iTotalDisplayRecords` variable correctly.

Add this below the "count existing records" section:

```
// { count records after filtering
$total_after_filter=$total_records;
if($search_sql){
    $r=dbRow("select count(ccode) as c from cities $search_sql");
    $total_after_filter=$r['c'];
}
// }
```

And we then also need to change the main query, and to add in the `iTotalDisplayRecords` to the opening of the returned JSON object:

```
echo
'{"iTotalRecords":'.$total_records.',
"iTotalDisplayRecords":'.$total_after_filter.',"aaData":[';
$rs=dbAll("select ccode,city,longitude,latitude
        from cities $search_sql
        order by $scol_name $sdir limit $start,$amt");
```

When that's complete, you can run queries in the browser. Here's an example run against my own **City**:

Country ▲	City ⇕	Latitude ⇕	Longitude ⇕
ie	monaghan	54.25	-6.96667
us	monaghan	34.8656	-82.4292

Show 10 entries   Search: monaghan

Showing 1 to 2 of 2 entries (filtered from 2673762 total entries)

If you run this yourself, you'll see that every time you hit a key, a query is sent to the server. As I've said earlier in the book, this is a very bad idea, which can cause race conditions and overloading on the server.

We'll solve that now.

Setting a delay on the filter

To avoid overloading your server, you need to query the data only when you've actually finished typing.

The DataTables plugin itself can be extended with further plugins, one of which is called fnSetFilteringDelay, created by Zygimantas Berziunas, which delays the sending of the query until after you've stopped typing.

To include it, simply copy and paste from the DataTables plugins page into your tables.html page, above the $(document).ready section, and then activate it by chaining it to your dataTable call.

Here is the JavaScript in full, with comments removed from the fnSetFilteringDelay plugin for readability (the license for the plugin is GPL2 or BSD3.x):

```
jQuery.fn.dataTableExt.oApi.fnSetFilteringDelay =
                                    function ( oSettings, iDelay ) {
    iDelay  = (iDelay && (/^[0-9]+$/.test(iDelay))) ? iDelay : 250;
    var $this = this, oTimerId;
    var anControl = $( 'div.dataTables_filter input:text' );
    anControl.unbind( 'keyup' ).bind( 'keyup', function() {
        var $$this = $this;
        window.clearTimeout(oTimerId);
        oTimerId = window.setTimeout(function() {
            $$this.fnFilter( anControl.val() );
        }, iDelay);
    });
    return this;
}
$(document).ready(function(){
    $('#the_table').dataTable({
        'bProcessing':true,
        'bServerSide':true,
        'sAjaxSource':'get_data.php'
    }).fnSetFilteringDelay();
});
```

What it does, is to remove keyup event of DataTables from the search box, and replace it with a less eager version, which will wait until you are finished typing before sending off the query.

Summary

In this chapter, we have learned how to display data using a plugin that allows the data to be sorted, searched, and paginated.

In the next chapter, we will discuss various ways to optimize jQuery and some other elements of the web development environment.

10
Optimization

Optimization in web development can mean many things. Optimization, in general, means to speed things up. There are a number of areas where we can speed things up in PHP and jQuery development.

Throughout the book, we have already seen some examples of optimization, without using the word to define it. Here are a few of them:

- Using plugins to provide functionality optimizes your own time, as you do not need to rewrite everything
- Using JSON instead of XML optimizes bandwidth and also reduces the amount of work needed by the server and client as they translate the data into their respective native object forms
- Using jQuery's Ajax methods instead of reloading every web page optimizes the user's experience, making interactions much snappier and faster

There are many other points, but these probably are the most obvious.

In this chapter, we'll look at some more methods to optimize your own time, and to make things even faster on the client.

We will look at:

- Creating a plugin
- Speeding up the page's rendering
- Avoiding out-of-date caches
- Speeding up CSS selectors

We'll also look at a lot of miscellaneous tips.

Optimizing the page load

Here is a very simple HTML file, which loads up five separate external JavaScript files:

```
<html>
  <head>
    <script src="jquery.min.js"></script>
    <script src="jquery-ui.min.js"></script>
    <script src="js.js"></script>
    <script src="scroller.js"></script>
    <script src="jquery.lazyload.mini.js"></script>
  </head>
  <body>
    finished loading
  </body>
</html>
```

When we check this in Firebug with a cleared cache, this is the graph of network activity we obtain:

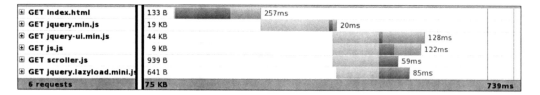

The various colors of each bar represent different stages of the request. The important part to note is the light gray on the extreme right end of each bar — that's the time spent on actually receiving the file. The rest is spent looking up the server, requesting the file, and waiting around for the server to respond.

In total, the preceding snapshot took 739 seconds for the browser to finish loading and render it on the screen. This may seem reasonable, but that's almost a full second until the words "Finished loading" are shown, on what is after all a very simple and small piece of HTML. Ideally, on a page with so little source text, you would hope for the "Finished loading" message to be displayed almost immediately.

Place scripts at the bottom

The first optimization that could be done is a visual one. If the page is displayed quickly, then people tend to believe that the page has finished loading quickly.

The quickest way to get the "Finished loading" message is to place the script inclusions at the bottom of the HTML instead of placing them at the top:

```html
<html>
  <head>
  </head>
  <body>
    finished loading
    <script src="jquery.min.js"></script>
    <script src="jquery-ui.min.js"></script>
    <script src="js.js"></script>
    <script src="scroller.js"></script>
    <script src="jquery.lazyload.mini.js"></script>
  </body>
</html>
```

This may appear to be a very minor change, but because the "Finished loading" message is now displayed before the scripts even start loading, the page appears to load in 257 ms instead of 739 ms. Just by moving the scripts, we've apparently tripled the speed of the page load.

That's still not perfect, as the scripts still need to actually finish downloading and run.

Aggregate and cache your scripts

Again, in the graph, we can see that most of the time is spent in requesting the files. We can reduce that by aggregating the files.

Programmers are usually recommended to fragment their files—for example, to only have one class per file, or to keep the model, view, and controller in totally separate files so that they are easier to manage.

Unfortunately, that's not a good strategy when the individual files need to be downloaded over a network. The lag between requesting and receiving a file is what causes a lot of web pages to appear to load slowly.

The easiest way to aggregate your scripts, without physically combining them, is to write a script. Let's call it getjs.php. Here is an example:

```php
<?php
header('Cache-Control: max-age=2592000, public');
header('Expires-Active: On');
header('Expires: Fri, 1 Jan 2500 01:01:01 GMT');
header('Pragma:');
header('Content-type: text/javascript; charset=utf-8');
echo file_get_contents('jquery.min.js');
```

```
echo file_get_contents('jquery-ui.min.js');
echo file_get_contents('js.js');
echo file_get_contents('scroller.js');
echo file_get_contents('jquery.lazyload.mini.js');
?>
```

The headers tell the browser to cache the downloaded file as long as possible, so that loading the page a second time should be even quicker.

Again, take a look at the sample network graph (with a cleared cache):

⊞ GET index.html	98 B	239ms		
⊞ GET getjs.php	74 KB		341ms	
2 requests	**74 KB**			**639ms**

It's not dramatic, but we've cut the download time of the full page in this instance by about 100 ms; over 10% quicker than the original.

It must be said that getting reliable and consistent network statistics is very difficult. Each load will be different because of other people on the network, or the server's hard drive being busy on another request, or your own machine being busy cleaning up memory. There are a number of things that will affect it.

To reliably know whether something works or not, you should actually try it out a few hundred times, preferably with a script.

Output HTML similar to the post-jQuery code

If a website is displayed quickly, people believe it has loaded completely, even if there are still some parts downloading in the background.

If you have a jQuery script that changes the appearance of an element after it has loaded, it can be a jarring experience for the user if their page suddenly changes appearance after it has been loaded.

You can get rid of this jarring event by outputting HTML in the first place that looks like the end product.

Optimizing development and maintenance

When people think of optimization, usually what they think of is ways to make the client-side script faster or ways to speed up the display of the page.

But, before the application gets that far, you need to write it. Here are a few tips for helping with parts of the development.

Writing your own plugins

The most important thing that any developer can do after completing a project is to look back and see what can be re-used for other systems.

This usually involves taking something that is specific to a task, and making it a little more general.

Looking back through this book, an example of this is the code we wrote in Chapter 4, *Forms and Form Validation*, to handle very large select boxes.

To recap, the problem outlined was that forms sometimes have very large select boxes to handle things like lists of pages, lists of countries, and so on. However, in many of those cases, the select box will not need to be changed. You might have opened an edit form to change a single value, for example, and no need to change any others.

And so it is a waste of processing and bandwidth to generate the unneeded options. We could save anywhere from milliseconds up to tens of seconds by sending only a single option for each select box and have the user retrieve the rest dynamically when they actually click on the box.

The example we looked at was of a country, but this kind of idea can obviously be expanded to many other purposes.

jQuery plugins are not difficult to write. They mostly follow the same basic pattern:

```
(function($){
  $.fn.yourpluginname=function(options){
    var opts=$.extend({},$.fn.yourpluginname.defaults,options);
    return this.each(function(){
      var $this=$(this);
      // place your code here
    });
  };
  $.fn.yourpluginname.defaults={
    // default values go here
  };
})(jQuery);
```

The above code is quite compact. What it does is to add a plugin called `yourpluginname` to jQuery, which you can then apply to any element.

Taking the code from Chapter 4, we can generalize it and create a plugin from it:

```
(function($){
  $.fn.remoteselectoptions=function(options){
    var opts=$.extend(
      {},
      $.fn.remoteselectoptions.defaults,options
    );
    if(!opts.url) return alert('no "url" parameter provided');
    return this.each(function(){
      var $this=$(this);
      $this.focus(function(){
        if($('option',$this).length>1) return;
        var v=$this.val();
        $.get(opts.url,{'selected':v},function(res){
          $this.html(res);
          setTimeout(function(){
            var options=$('option',$this);
            for(var i=0,found=0;i<options.length,!found;++i){
              if(options[i].value!=v) continue;
              $this.attr('selectedIndex',i);
              found=1;
            }
          },1);
        });
      });
    });
  };
  $.fn.remoteselectoptions.defaults={
    'url':null
  };
})(jQuery);
```

If you compare this to the code in Chapter 4, you'll see its programming logic is virtually the same, but the code has been made more generic, and the separate `form_setCountries` function has been incorporated as an inline function (beginning on the `$.get()` line) and expanded to be more robust.

Let's say you have a select box named *countries* and you have a list of countries in a text file named `countries.txt`, already in `<option>` form; you might place this in your HTML form:

```
<select name="countries"><option>Ireland</option></select>
```

And in your `$(document).ready`, you would put this:

```
$('select[name=countries]').remoteselectoptions({
  url:'countries.txt'
});
```

By creating a plugin out of the code, we have now made it very easy and efficient for future forms to be optimized in exactly the same way.

Un-caching your JavaScript

Imagine you have a homepage named `index.php`, which reads a script named `gallery.js` containing this:

```
function sho_gallery(){
  // insert code here
}
$(document).ready(show_gallery);
```

And using our previous section for guidance, you are aggregating the script through `getjs.php`, along with your other scripts. After the script has been up on your site for a few hours and people have already seen it, you get a call saying that the gallery is not working.

You immediately correct the misspelled function name and call the person back. That person then views the site and says that it is still not working. Obviously, the viewer's browser has cached the old incorrect version.

This is a very common scenario, and in a case where there may be hundreds of readers an hour, or many repeat visitors who may have cached versions days or weeks old, it can be a daunting task to get them to clear their caches and reload.

There is a very simple solution, though.

The usual way to link to the `getjs.php` script would be this:

```
<script src="getjs.php"></script>
```

But because with PHP, you can place a slash after the `.php` extension followed by other characters and the script will still be called, we have a new option, which is to add an MD5 to the script name, based on the modified date of the files.

```
<?php
  $dir='.'; // directory containing the scripts
  $d=0;
  foreach (new DirectoryIterator($dir) as $file) {
```

```
        $d+=$file->getMTime();
    }
?>
<script src="getjs.php/<?php echo md5($d); ?>"></script>
```

What this does is to add up the times that the files were last modified, and create an MD5 from that, which is added to the end of the script's filename.

For example:

```
<script src="getjs.php/873cf14a728d065d96f009bedde74ea7"></script>
```

The script name is cacheable, as it does not contain a query mark, and as long as no files are changed in the directory, the MD5 will not change either.

This time, when someone says there is an error on the page, you fix it, and when the caller checks the page again, the MD5 changes and a new copy of the script is downloaded.

The really important thing about this is that at all stages, the result is cacheable. All that's changing is how the getjs.php file is referenced.

This is a form of optimization, in that you are making sure that bug-fixes are disseminated immediately, instead of whenever the client refreshes their cache or the cache times out.

Optimizing jQuery

When writing jQuery code, there are a number of things you can do to get better response times from the client.

These tips are useful when you are doing heavy scripting on the client. If you use jQuery only for minor manipulations, then the user will probably not notice the difference, so these can probably be better considered "best practices" than essential time savers.

However, if you train yourself to always follow these tips, then your web page will run just about as fast as it can, and will probably not need to be improved.

Use Google's CDN

Every new release of jQuery is better and faster than the version before it. When you are starting a new project, you should always check to see if there is a new version available.

A way to stay up to date without much effort is to use Google's **CDN (Content Delivery Network)**, which keeps copies of popular libraries such as jQuery, MooTools, and Dojo among others.

A CDN is a network of computers, which is spread around the world, so that files are delivered to their requesters from the closest server possible.

One very useful side effect of using a CDN is that, when someone comes to your website, they have probably already encountered a few websites using the CDN, so jQuery will already be cached in their browsers.

For more information on Google's CDN for jQuery, follow `http://code.google.com/apis/ajaxlibs/documentation/index.html#jquery`.

To use the CDN for your scripts, all you need to do is to replace your jQuery and jQuery UI `<script>` tags with these:

```
<script
  src="http://ajax.googleapis.com/ajax/libs/jquery/1/jquery.min.js">
</script>
<script
  src="http://ajax.googleapis.com/ajax/libs/jqueryui/1
                                          /jquery-ui.min.js">
</script>
<style type="text/css">
  @import "http://ajax.googleapis.com/ajax/libs/jqueryui/1/themes
                                  /smoothness/jquery-ui.css";
</style>
```

The files in the `/1/` directories are the latest 1.x files available. For example, if jQuery 1.4 or 1.5 comes out, then Google would upgrade the files in the `/jquery/1/` directory to match that.

If you want a specific copy of jQuery, you can access it using the Google CDN as well:

```
<script
  src="http://ajax.googleapis.com/ajax/libs/jquery/1.3.2
                                          /jquery.min.js">
</script>
<script
  src="http://ajax.googleapis.com/ajax/libs/jqueryui/1.7.2
                                          /jquery-ui.min.js">
</script>
<style type="text/css">
    @import "http://ajax.googleapis.com/ajax/libs/jqueryui/1.7.2
                                /themes/smoothness/jquery-ui.css";
</style>
```

Notice the 1.3.2 and 1.7.2 numbers. If version 1.4 of jQuery or 1.8 of jQuery UI comes out, the specific versions retrieved will still be 1.3.2 and 1.7.2.

Note, though, that if you are working on a project that might need to be offline at some point (for example, if it is an application that runs on your own laptop and you are not always online), then Google's CDN will not be available to you. In those cases, you should download a copy of the library from jQuery's website and keep it locally.

If you want to stay up to date with the new versions of jQuery added by Google, you should add their RSS feed to your reader, by subscribing at http://ajax-api-alerts.blogspot.com/feeds/posts/default?alt=rss.

Caching jQuery objects

If you know that you will need to perform a task on the same selected elements again, you should cache the jQuery object for later use.

So, instead of using the following:

```
$('.someclass').click(function(){
   alert('clicked');
});
// do some other stuff here before carrying on
$('.someclass').css('background','red')
   .text('some text');
```

You would use this:

```
var els=$('.someclass');
els.click(function(){
   alert('clicked');
});
// do some other stuff here before carrying on
els.css('background','red')
   .text('some text');
```

This makes sure you are not searching for the same stuff all the time.

When we write $('.someclass'), what it means is "Search for all the elements matching this selector, and give us the result wrapped in a jQuery object." If we do this every single time we do anything to these elements, we are doing a lot of searching! It does not make sense to run the same search over and over, so we assign the result to the variable els, and run consecutive commands on this variable instead of running the search again.

In PHP, this is commonly described by using the following:

```php
for($i=0;$i<count($arr);$i++){
   echo $arr[$i];
}
```

The problem with this piece of PHP code is that the `for` loop will run the `count()` function upon every iteration of the loop. It does not make sense to do so, and so it is wise to cache the value of the `count()` before starting the `for` loop:

```php
$c=count($arr);
for($i=0;$i<c;$i++){
   echo $arr[$i];
}
```

To take this idea a bit further, if you are doing the manipulations in a function that might be called a few times, you are better off caching the objects in a global cache, so that the function is not performing the search every time.

For example, this code will initialize a global cache with a copy of the `$('.someclass')` object:

```javascript
$(document).ready(function(){
   window.cache={
      'els':$('.someclass')
   };
});
```

And then when the objects are needed, instead of creating a new `$('.someclass')` instance, you re-use the cached one:

```javascript
function do_actions(){
   var els=window.$cache.els;
   els.click(function(){
      alert('clicked');
   });
   // do some other stuff here before carrying on
   els.css('background','red')
      .text('some text');
}
```

Note that this kind of caching is best used for element collections that will not be deleted from or added to throughout the page life. If you do need to add or delete something, you should reset the cached object as well, using something like this:

```javascript
$('.someclass').click(function(){
   $(this).remove();
   window.$cache.els=$('.someclass');
});
```

Use $.load for non-visual code

In the examples throughout the book, I've used $(document).ready to initialize most of the code.

The $.ready event binds a function to the document so that when it is "ready" to be manipulated (that is, it has downloaded enough of the source code to be sure no further HTML elements will be added to it), you can run your code. The $.load event is different from that, as it runs after everything in the page, including images, objects, and frames has been downloaded.

So, you should use $.ready if your code is visual and needs to be run as soon as possible so as to avoid flickering on the screen as the DOM is changed. And you should use $.load for non-visual code that will probably not be needed immediately while the user reads the page and figures out what they want to do. As an example, consider a form. With modern bandwidth speeds, it is very unlikely that a human will fill out a form before the rest of the page has downloaded, so it makes sense to attach form validation events to the form after images and other objects have downloaded. This leaves CPU cycles spare so that the more important visual code, such as tabs, accordions, data tables, and so on can be completed first.

For example, this code will add visual code as soon as possible, and form validation after the rest of the page has finished loading:

```
$(document).ready(function(){
    $('#tabs').tabs();
    $('#data').dataTable();
});
$(document).load(function(){
    $('#form1').validate();
});
```

JavaScript optimizations

The Javascript optimization tricks are not specific to jQuery, but are very good to know.

Chaining

Chaining means running a number of functions on a selected element or group of elements.

Consider what happens when you do this:

```
$('.someclass').click(function(){
  alert('clicked');
});
$('.someclass').css('background','red');
$('.someclass').text('some text');
```

On each line, jQuery is called with a fresh request to get all elements with the class name `someclass` and manipulate them in some way. This is quite expensive to do, as jQuery does not automatically cache the requests, so it's a fresh search every time.

To speed this up, you should chain the functions like this:

```
$('.someclass').click(function(){
  alert('clicked');
})
.css('background','red')
.text('some text');
```

This runs the selector search once, and then runs all three operations on the same object.

Speeding up selectors

Another thing to watch out for is the selector itself. Some types of selector run quicker than others.

Consider this snippet:

```
$('#id1').css('color','red');
$('span').css('color','red');
$('.class1').css('color','red');
```

These selectors are written in order of speed. The first is the fastest, and the third is the slowest.

The first selector runs very quickly because IDs are supposed to be unique identity tags for specific elements—as soon as the browser finds the first one, it stops looking for more.

For example, consider the following lines of code:

```
<div id="id1">test1</div><div id="id1">test2</div>
<script>
  $('#id1').css('color','red');
</script>
```

In this example, only the first `<div>` element will turn red.

The second selector is based on tag names, and will run quickly as well, because it can use a native DOM function, `getElementsByTagName`, to quickly retrieve the elements.

The third selector, though, is very slow in comparison to the others, especially in browsers that do not have a native `getElementsByClassName` function.

The reason for this is that the selector engine needs to check against absolutely every element in the document. To help this, you should use more specific selectors when possible. For example, if you know that the class name `class1` will only appear on `<span>` elements, then say so in the jQuery call as follows:

```
$('span.class1').css('color','red');
```

jQuery will now search by tag name first, finding all `<span>` elements, and then search those elements for the class name.

This is true not only of jQuery; you should do the same with your normal web-page CSS, especially if you have documents having hundreds or thousands of elements. The problem of selector querying speed is not just a jQuery problem.

Also, if you know that the elements are contained within an element or group of elements that you've already selected, you can include that as a second parameter, which will tell jQuery to search only within the pre-selected elements:

```
var container=$('#container');
// do manipulations on #container
$('span.class1',container).css('color','red');
```

Note the comment here—there's no point in selecting an element just to improve the following selection. CSS can handle most of the things you would want to implement natively. If no actions were performed on `#container` before it was used to narrow the search for `span.class1`, then the preceding code snippet would have been better written as this:

```
$('#container span.class1').css('color','red');
```

Inject multiple elements at once

When adding elements to the page, DOM manipulations can be very slow—every time an element is added, the browser needs to re-calculate the sizes (padding, margin, width, height, and so on) of every visible element before re-displaying the screen.

This means that if you add 100 elements to the page, one after the other, then the browser will refresh its model 100 times, which can slow down your script.

To prevent this, you should first build all of your elements in memory using an array, and then add them all at once to the page so that it needs to refresh only once. For example, if you are adding 100 list elements to a `<ul>` container, your code might look like this:

```
var ul=$('<ul></ul>').appendTo($('#ul_goes_here'));
for(var i=0;i<100;++i)$('<li>'+i+'</li>').appendTo(ul);
```

After a number of tests, you'll find that this averages to about 195 ms to run in the browser (using the Profile tool in Firebug). But, you can see a number of DOM operations going on there. Let's rewrite it to have only one DOM operation:

```
var lis=[];
for(var i=0;i<100;++i)lis[i]='<li>'+i+'</li>';
$('<ul>'+lis.join('')+'</ul>').appendTo($('#ul_goes_here'));
```

Now, this averages to about 14 ms to run, instead of 195 ms. That's more than 10 times quicker.

Note the usage of a JavaScript array here, and the join at the end. That's a small optimization trick that is common to PHP as well. It is always quicker to join than to concatenate.

Another note is that in this example, we created a `<ul>` element and populated it. As a result, the `<ul>` is created in memory and the `<li>` elements are added to it, and then the `<ul>` is added to the page using a single DOM operation.

Had the `<ul>` already existed in the page and we needed to add the `<li>` elements to that pre-created element, we would have got 100 operations. So, always try to inject just one element. If you have a lot of elements to be injected, add a wrapper element around them. For example, if you are adding a few `<p>` elements, you might add them to a container `<div>` and append the `<div>` to the page as one operation, instead of appending each `<p>` individually.

Using setTimeout

`setTimeout` helps to smooth the user experience. I have a number of projects where I do some very heavy processing in JavaScript.

In most browsers, the JavaScript engine is not threaded. This means that when the JavaScript engine is busy, the browser does not respond to user actions. You may have seen this yourself, where some pages will simply stop responding for almost half a minute, then an alert will pop up saying that a script is making the page slow.

As a programmer, it's your responsibility to make sure that the page response is quick and smooth. This can be tricky when the browser locks up on long scripts.

As an example, let's consider this simple piece of code:

```
<html>
  <head>
    <script>
      function do_it(){
        for(var i=0;i<1000000;++i){
          window.status='number:'+i;
        }
      }
    </script>
  </head>
  <body>
    <a href="javascript:do_it()">do it</a>
  </body>
</html>
```

On my computer, the entire browser locks up and the `window.status` changes can't be seen until the loop is about half way done, when the browser offers to kill it.

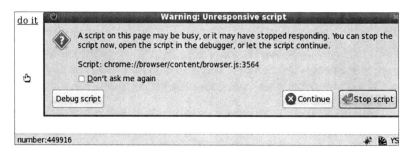

To solve this kind of problem, we need to periodically give control of the page back to the browser itself.

To do this, you should take the large loops, and break them into smaller chunks that can be paused every now and then and resumed a few milliseconds later.

```
function do_it(start){
  var i=start || 0;
  for(;i<1000000,i<start+1000;++i){
    window.status='number:'+i;
  }
  if(i<1000000)setTimeout("do_it("+i+");",10);
}
```

Now, when the **do it** link is clicked, you can see things progressing smoothly, and if you want to click on buttons or go to different tabs or perform any other browser action, you can do so.

The 10 millisecond delay allows the browser enough time to refresh any changed content, or respond to user events.

The `var i=start || 0;` statement is an alternative to the `var i=start?start:0;` statement. However, it's very mildly faster.

Use var for your variables

Here is an example of JavaScript that does not use the `var` keyword:

```
function test(){
  for(i=0;i<100;++i){
    j=i+1;
    window.status=j;
  }
}
```

When `i` is set to `0`, and when `j` is set, the browser does not know if the variable being referred to is new or is a global variable. So, it "bubbles up" the scope chain, checking outside the `for` loop, then outside the function, until it finds a reference to it or it gets to the window level and stops.

In the cases of variables `i` and `j`, this is a waste of CPU, as we know these refer to local variables but the browser doesn't and must check all the way up the scope chain. In the case of `window.status`, it's the desired behavior, as we are setting a global variable.

If you want really fast JavaScript, you should get into the habit of declaring your variables as follows:

```
function test(){
  for(var i=0;i<100;++i){
    var j=i+1;
    window.status=j;
  }
}
```

Another reason to do this is to let **minifier** scripts such as YUI Compressor optimize variable names while compressing their scripts. You can get Yahoo's minifier from `http://developer.yahoo.com/yui/compressor/`.

A **minifier** is a script that is run on JavaScript or CSS to remove all extraneous spaces or comments so that it can be downloaded as quickly as possible.

Some minifiers even rename variables with shorter versions.

In order to ensure your scripts work properly after they've been minified, you need to be very careful that you have declared all variables, placed semicolons at the end of each line, and so on.

Yet another reason is to avoid errors.

As an example, let's say you have this function:

```javascript
function show_doc(){
   document='report.doc';
   alert(document);
}
```

This will not work as you might expect, you'll end up getting a screen similar to the following:

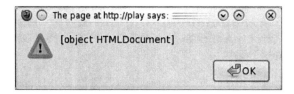

As the `document` variable is already set in the global scope as a reference to the page itself, the function tries to set the entire page equal to a string, which obviously should not be allowed.

To correct it, simply place `var` before the `document` variable to declare it as a local variable:

```javascript
function show_doc(){
   var document='report.doc';
   alert(document);
}
```

Now when it is run, you get the expected alert:

Summary

In this chapter, we looked at some ways of optimizing the user experience, the developer experience, and some methods of speeding up scripts and loading time.

We saw that optimization is not strictly about making the client side faster, but in a lot of ways is about making your own work, as a developer, more efficient.

I hope you enjoyed the book, and found a few new and interesting tricks that you will use in your work. If you enjoyed what you saw of jQuery, then I recommend that you read into it a bit more by buying the book *Learning jQuery 1.3* published by *Packt Publishing*.

Index

resizing, on client side 128
resizing, on server side 129

F

file
  Ajax-based file uploads 109
  client-side code 109-112
  confirmation message, changing in
      fm_deleteDirectory function 115
  deleting 113
  downloading 116
  downloading, client-side code 116, 117
  downloading, on server side 117
  else clause, adding 114
  fm_runAction function, modifying 114
  moving 113
  renaming 113
  server-side code, modifying 115, 116
  server-side code, writing 112, 113
  Uploadify plugin, adding 109
  uploading 109
file management
  about 93
  directory, choosing 95
  directory, creating 100
  directory, deleting 100
  directory, moving 105
  directory, renaming 100
  file, deleting 113
  file, downloading 116
  file, moving 113
  file, renaming 113
  file, uploading 109
  security 93
filtering
  about 201
  on server-side code 201, 202
  sSearch parameters 201
fm_changeOptions function
  about 108
  changes, incorporating 110
fm_getFiles function 107
fm_updateValues function 97, 107
fnSetFilteringDelay
  using, for query delay 203

form validation
  jQuery validation plugin, using 74
  setting up, in PHP 78
  using 73
form validation, setting up in PHP
  server-side code, validating 78

G

get_errors function 80
get_manipulated_image function 162

H

hierarchical tree, sorting
  about 175
  client-side code 175-181
  HTML example, creating 175, 176
  server-side code 181, 182
  sorting-trees.js file 176, 177

I

iColumns parameter 198
iDisplayLength parameter 198
iDisplayStart parameter 198
image
  caching, on client side 156
  caching, on server side 157, 159
  client-side code, adding to file 148, 149
  cropping, on client side 163, 165
  cropping, on server side 166
  image.php file 146
  images_libs.php file, creating 148
  list, displaying 146
  manipulating, with PHP 151
  resizing 159
  resizing, on client side 160, 161
  resizing, on server side 162
  saving, on client side 156
  saving, on server side 157, 159
  selecting 149
  selecting. client-side code 149, 150
  selecting. server-side code 150, 151
  Treeview widget, using 146
  using 145

SQL injection 73
sSearch_(int)parameter 198
sSearch parameter 198
switch block 105

T

tab
  about 43
  client-side code 63
  content 45
  defining, special codes used 61
  list 44, 45
  panels, loading through Ajax 69-71
  server-side code 63- 65
  special codes, visual explanation 62
  visual difference 43
tab panels 69-71
tab, server-side management
  about 58
  server-side code 58
  server-side code, converting 59
  server-side code, data display 60, 61

U

ui parameter 68
Unobtrusive JavaScript
  example 55

V

validate plugin 75, 76
validation
  client side 73
  server side 73

W

WordPress, PHP 16

X

XML 13
XMLHTTPRequest object 14

Z

zindex 138
zipped package, jQuery validation plugin
  downloading 74

Packt Open Source Project Royalties

When we sell a book written on an Open Source project, we pay a royalty directly to that project. Therefore by purchasing jQuery 1.3 with PHP, Packt will have given some of the money received to the jQuery project.

In the long term, we see ourselves and you — customers and readers of our books — as part of the Open Source ecosystem, providing sustainable revenue for the projects we publish on. Our aim at Packt is to establish publishing royalties as an essential part of the service and support a business model that sustains Open Source.

If you're working with an Open Source project that you would like us to publish on, and subsequently pay royalties to, please get in touch with us.

Writing for Packt

We welcome all inquiries from people who are interested in authoring. Book proposals should be sent to author@packtpub.com. If your book idea is still at an early stage and you would like to discuss it first before writing a formal book proposal, contact us; one of our commissioning editors will get in touch with you.

We're not just looking for published authors; if you have strong technical skills but no writing experience, our experienced editors can help you develop a writing career, or simply get some additional reward for your expertise.

About Packt Publishing

Packt, pronounced 'packed', published its first book "Mastering phpMyAdmin for Effective MySQL Management" in April 2004 and subsequently continued to specialize in publishing highly focused books on specific technologies and solutions.

Our books and publications share the experiences of your fellow IT professionals in adapting and customizing today's systems, applications, and frameworks. Our solution-based books give you the knowledge and power to customize the software and technologies you're using to get the job done. Packt books are more specific and less general than the IT books you have seen in the past. Our unique business model allows us to bring you more focused information, giving you more of what you need to know, and less of what you don't.

Packt is a modern, yet unique publishing company, which focuses on producing quality, cutting-edge books for communities of developers, administrators, and newbies alike. For more information, please visit our website: www.PacktPub.com.

jQuery UI 1.6
The User Interface Library for jQuery

Build highly interactive web applications with ready-to-use widgets from the jQuery user interface library

Dan Wellman

PACKT

jQuery UI 1.6: The User Interface Library for jQuery

ISBN: 978-1-847195-12-8   Paperback: 440 pages

Build highly interactive web applications with ready-to-use widgets of the jQuery user interface library

1. Packed with examples and clear explanations to easily design elegant and powerful front-end interfaces for your web applications

2. Organize your interfaces with reusable widgets like accordions, date pickers, dialogs, sliders, tabs, and more

3. Enhance the interactivity of your pages by making elements drag and droppable, sortable, selectable, and resizable

Drupal 6 JavaScript and jQuery

Putting jQuery, AJAX, and JavaScript effects into your Drupal 6 modules and themes

Matt Butcher

PACKT

Drupal 6 JavaScript and jQuery

ISBN: 978-1-847196-16-3   Paperback: 340 pages

Putting jQuery, AJAX, and JavaScript effects into your Drupal 6 modules and themes

1. Learn about JavaScript support in Drupal 6

2. Packed with example code ready for you to use

3. Harness the popular jQuery library to enhance your Drupal sites

4. Make the most of Drupal's built-in JavaScript libraries

Please check **www.PacktPub.com** for information on our titles

Learning jQuery 1.3

ISBN: 978-1-847196-70-5   Paperback: 444 pages

Better Interaction Design and Web Development with Simple JavaScript Techniques

1. An introduction to jQuery that requires minimal programming experience

2. Detailed olutions to specific client-side problems

3. For web designers to create interactive elements for their designs

4. For developers to create the best user interface for their web applications

RESTful PHP Web Services

ISBN: 978-1-847195-52-4   Paperback: 220 pages

Learn the basic architectural concepts and step through examples of consuming and creating RESTful web services in PHP

1. Get familiar with REST principles

2. Learn how to design and implement PHP web services with REST

3. Real-world examples, with services and client PHP code snippets

Please check **www.PacktPub.com** for information on our titles

Breinigsville, PA USA
13 November 2009
227409BV00003B/2/P